Quick Reference

Que Quick Reference Series

STEVE DAVIS

dBASE IV 1.5 Quick Reference

Library of Congress Catalog Number: 92-70874

ISBN: 0-88022-905-5

95 94 93 92 4 3 2

Interpretation of the printing code: the rightmost double-digit number is the year of the book's printing; the rightmost single-digit number is the number of the book's printing. For example, a printing code of 92-1 shows that the first printing of the book occurred in 1992.

CREDITS

Publisher
Lloyd J. Short

Acquisitions Editor
Tim Ryan

Production Editor
Jill D. Bond

Technical Editor
Erik McBeth

Production Team
Bob LaRoche, Laurie Lee, Anne Owen, Juli Pavey, Susan VandeWalle, Lisa Wilson, Allan Wimmer, Phil Worthington

TRADEMARK ACKNOWLEDGMENTS

dBASE is a registered trademark of Ashton-Tate Corporation.

Lotus 1-2-3 is a registered trademark of Lotus Development Corporation.

PFS:File is a registered trademark of Spinnaker Software Corporation.

RapidFile is a trademark of Ashton-Tate Corporation.

Framework is a registered trademark of Ashton-Tate Corporation.

TABLE OF CONTENTS

Introduction ix

COMMAND REFERENCE 1

= 1
?,??,??? 1
! 3
*, && 3
@...SAY, GET 3
@...TO, FILL, CLEAR, SCROLL 5
ACCEPT 6
ACTIVATE MENU 7
ACTIVATE POPUP 7
ACTIVATE SCREEN 7
ACTIVATE WINDOW 8
APPEND 8
APPEND FROM 9
APPEND MEMO 11
ASSIST 12
AVERAGE 12
BEGIN/END TRANS 13
BLANK 14
BROWSE 15
CALCULATE 17
CALL 18
CANCEL 19
CHANGE 21
CLEAR 21
CLOSE 22
COMPILE 23
CONTINUE 24

CONVERT 24
COPY 25
COUNT 27
CREATE APPLICATION 27
CREATE FROM 28
CREATE/MODIFY LABEL 29
CREATE/MODIFY QUERY/VIEW 30
CREATE/MODIFY REPORT 32
CREATE/MODIFY SCREEN 33
CREATE or MODIFY STRUCTURE 35
DEACTIVATE MENU 36
DEACTIVATE POPUP 36
DEACTIVATE WINDOW 36
DEBUG 36
DECLARE 37
DEFINE BAR 38
DEFINE BOX 38
DEFINE MENU, DEFINE PAD 39
DEFINE POPUP 41
DEFINE WINDOW 42
DELETE 44
DELETE FILE 45
DELETE TAG 45
DEXPORT 46
DIR 47
DISPLAY 48
DO 48
DO CASE, ENDCASE 49
DO WHILE, ENDDO 50
EDIT 51
EJECT, EJECT PAGE 53
ERASE 54
EXPORT 55
FIND 57
FUNCTION 58
GO, GOTO 59
HELP 60
IF, ENDIF 61
IMPORT 63
INDEX 64

INPUT 65
INSERT 66
JOIN 66
KEYBOARD 68
LABEL FORM 68
LIST 69
LOAD 71
LOCATE 72
LOGOUT 73
MODIFY APPLICATION 73
MODIFY COMMAND/FILE 74
MODIFY LABEL 74
MODIFY QUERY/VIEW 75
MODIFY REPORT 75
MODIFY SCREEN 75
MODIFY STRUCTURE 75
MOVE WINDOW 75
NOTE 75
ON ERROR, ESCAPE, KEY 76
ON PAD 77
ON PAGE 78
ON READERROR 78
ON SELECTION PAD 79
ON SELECTION POPUP 79
PACK 79
PARAMETERS 79
PLAY MACRO 81
PRINTJOB/ENDPRINTJOB 82
PRIVATE 83
PROCEDURE 85
PROTECT 85
PUBLIC 87
QUIT 87
READ 88
RECALL 88
REINDEX 89
RELEASE 89
RENAME 90
REPLACE 91
REPLACE FROM ARRAY 93

REPORT FORM 94
RESET 95
RESTORE 96
RESUME 97
RETRY 98
RETURN 99
ROLLBACK 100
RUN/! 101
SAVE 102
SCAN, ENDSCAN 103
SEEK 104
SELECT 106
SET 107
SHOW MENU 112
SHOW POPUP 112
SKIP 112
SORT 113
STORE 114
SUM 117
SUSPEND 117
TEXT, ENDTEXT 118
TOTAL 119
TYPE 120
UNLOCK 121
UPDATE 122
USE 123
WAIT 124
ZAP 125

dBASE IV FUNCTIONS 126

LOW-LEVEL FILE I/O FUNCTIONS 137

SQL COMMAND REFERENCE 139
SQL FUNCTIONS 142

Index 145

INTRODUCTION

dBASE IV 1.5 Quick Reference covers all dBASE commands, dBASE functions, and SQL functions so that you can use this powerful package effectively. In this book, each dBASE IV command is presented in the same format: the purpose appears first, followed by reminders, proper syntax, step-by-step procedures, and a "Notes" section that contains additional comments and hints. Cautions are given for some commands.

In the statement of syntax, the command appears in all uppercase and in blue, such as **COMMAND**. Variable information appears in lowercase italic enclosed in angle brackets—such as, <*information*>. Do not type the brackets when you enter the information. Optional interior commands appear in uppercase enclosed in brackets—such as, [COMMAND]. Do not type the brackets when you enter the command.

This book lists numbered steps for commands that can be used from the Control Center. Steps from the Control Center are not listed when a command cannot be accessed from the Control Center.

COMMAND REFERENCE

=

See *STORE*.

?,??,???

Purpose

Displays information on the screen or printer with the ?, ?? commands. Sends special codes to the printer with the ??? command.

Command Syntax

?/?? [*<expression-1>* [PICTURE "*<clause>*"]
[FUNCTION "*<function-list>*"] [AT *<expN>*]
[STYLE *<font-number>*]] [,*<expression-2>*,...]

??? *<control-character>*

From the dot prompt

1. Issue the **?** command when you want to display an expression or value on the next line. The **??** command displays the expression without advancing to the next line.
2. Send printer commands without moving the print head with the **???** commands. The following commands are for an EPSON printer. Check your printer manual for the correct font codes.

```
??? chr(15)
? "Test of condensed print."
STYLE "B"
??? chr(18)
? "Back to normal size." STYLE "I"
```

Notes

Include the CHR () function in the ??? command line.

Control the style of output with STYLE. Enclose any style options in double quotes. The style options are Bold, Subscript, Underline, Italic, and Superscript (B, L, U, I, and R).

Control the format of output with the following functions:

Function	Description
H <*n*>	Stretches a field horizontally a maximum of *n* columns.
V <*n*>	Stretches a field vertically a maximum of *n* rows.
B	Left-aligns text within a field.
I	Centers text within a field.
J	Right-aligns text within a field.

Function	Description
T	Trims leading and trailing blanks.
$	Displays a floating currency symbol before or after a numeric field. The position of the symbol is controlled with SET CURRENCY LEFT or RIGHT.
L	Displays numeric fields with leading zeros.

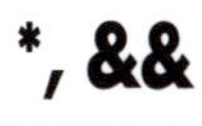

See *RUN/!*.

See *NOTE*.

@...SAY, GET

Purpose

Positions the cursor or information on the screen or printer page.

Command Syntax

@ <*row*>,<*col*> [SAY <*expression*> [PICTURE "<*clause*>"] [FUNCTION "<*function-list*>"]] [GET <*variable*> [[OPEN] WINDOW <*window-name*>] [PICTURE"<*clause*>"] [FUNCTION "<*function-list*>"] [RANGE [REQUIRED]

<low>,*<high>*] [VALID [REQUIRED] *<condition>* [ERROR *<expC>*]] [WHEN *<condition>*] [DEFAULT *<expression>*] [MESSAGE *<expC*]] [COLOR [*<standard>*] [,*<enhanced>*]]

From the dot prompt

1. Use the **@...SAY** command to position and display screen and printer information. A SET DEVICE TO PRINTER command causes all following @...SAY commands to be sent to the printer. SET DEVICE TO SCREEN redirects @...SAY commands back to the screen.
2. The **@...GET** command specifies an input area for user input. Restrict the size and type of input with the **PICTURE** clause.
3. Use the **DEFAULT** option to suggest a preset value for a @...GET.
4. Use the **ERROR** option to specify a custom error message. The default error message is `Editing condition not satisfied.`

From the Control Center

Create a screen form to position information.

Notes

Most monitors have 24 lines down and 80 columns across. An 8 1/2-by-11-inch page allows 66 lines down and 80 columns across in normal print font and 75 lines down and 132 columns across in condensed font.

Line 22 is unavailable if SET STATUS is set to ON. Line 0 is unavailable if SET SCOREBOARD is set to ON.

Remember to redirect output back to the screen with the SET DEVICE TO SCREEN command after a

SET DEVICE TO PRINT command, or screen information will be sent to the printer.

@...TO, FILL, CLEAR, SCROLL

Purpose

Outlines, colors, clears, or shifts contents of areas on-screen. Use this technique to customize screen appearance.

Command Syntax

@<row-1>,*<col-1>* **TO** *<row-2>,<col-2>* [DOUBLE/PANEL/*<border-definition-string>*] [COLOR *<color-attribute>*]

@*<row-1>,<col-1>* **FILL TO** *<row-2>,<col-2>* [COLOR *<color-attribute>*]

@*<row-1>,<col-1>* **CLEAR** [TO *<row-2>,<col-2>*]

@ *<row-1>,<col-1>* **TO** *<row-2>,<col-2>* **SCROLL** [UP/DOWN/LEFT/RIGHT] [BY <expN>] [WRAP]

From the dot prompt

The following commands draw and fill a box on-screen:

```
@ 08,15 to 14,60 double color r/w
```

```
@ 09,16 fill to 13,59 color w/n
```

From the Control Center

1. Select the Create option from the Forms column of the Control Center.

2. Select the Layout/Box/Double options to draw a double-line box.

3. Anchor the upper left corner of the box by positioning the cursor at the desired location and pressing **Enter**. Stretch the box with the arrow keys and press **Enter** to complete it.

4. Press **F6** to select the box.

5. Press **F1**. Select the Words/Display submenus.

   Use the arrow keys to move to the color you want and press **Enter** to select it. Do this for foreground as well as background colors.

   Press **Ctrl-End** to select the color combination and exit the submenus.

Note

Avoid overlaying information that the user needs to keep on-screen.

ACCEPT

Purpose

Stops program activity and asks the user for information.

Command Syntax

ACCEPT [<*prompt*>] **TO** <*memvar*>

From the dot prompt

Issue the **ACCEPT** command from the dot prompt or in a program.

Notes

Use the ACCEPT command to create character or numeric data type variables.

The INPUT and WAIT commands also stop program processing until the user responds.

When you use the ACCEPT, INPUT, or WAIT commands, you cannot control the user's response.

ACTIVATE MENU

See *DEFINE MENU/DEFINE PAD.*

ACTIVATE POPUP

See *DEFINE POPUP.*

ACTIVATE SCREEN

Purpose

Enables the entire screen, rather than a predefined window, to be used or active. Other windows may be scrolled or cleared from the screen.

Command Syntax

ACTIVATE SCREEN

From the dot prompt

Write a program and include a combination of the windowing command lines.

```
DEFINE WINDOW Test from 3,5 to 10,50
ACTIVATE WINDOW Test
   ? "This is the Active window."
ACTIVATE SCREEN
CLEAR
```

The ACTIVATE SCREEN command line causes the window to stretch and cover the whole screen.

Note

Other window commands are: DEFINE WINDOW, ACTIVATE WINDOW, DEACTIVATE WINDOW, MOVE WINDOW, SAVE WINDOW, RESTORE WINDOW, and RELEASE WINDOW.

ACTIVATE WINDOW

See *DEFINE WINDOW*.

APPEND

Purpose

Adds records to a dBASE IV datafile.

Command Syntax

APPEND [BLANK][BLANK]/[NOORGANIZE]

From the dot prompt

1. Open the datafile by issuing the USE command.

2. Type APPEND and press Enter. A blank record appears on-screen. This is called the Append mode.
3. Type the data in each area of the blank record. When the record is filled, another blank record becomes available.
4. Press Ctrl-End to exit Append Mode.

From the Control Center

1. Position the bounce bar on a file and press Enter to select it.
2. When asked, select the Display Data option.
3. From the Records menu, select Add New Records.

Notes

Press PgUp and PgDn to move to the preceding and next record. End the append activity by pressing Ctrl-End.

All new records are added to the end of the datafile.

APPEND FROM

Purpose

Adds records to a database from an array or another database.

Command Syntax

APPEND FROM ARRAY <*array-name*> [REINDEX]
[FOR <*condition*>]

APPEND FROM *<file-name>*/?[[TYPE] *<file-type>*] [REINDEX] [FOR *<condition>*]

From the dot prompt

1. Before you use the APPEND FROM ARRAY command, make sure that the array has been declared and filled with information.
2. Issue the **APPEND FROM** command to get information from another file.

From the Control Center

1. Position the bounce bar on a file and press **Enter** to select it.
2. When asked, select the Modify Structure/Order option.
3. Use the arrow keys to open the Append submenu and select an option.
4. Choose either Append Records from dBASE File or Copy Records from non-dBASE File.

Notes

The array elements of information must be in the same order as the record structure. The first array element value is moved to the first field in the record, and so on. dBASE IV ignores extra array elements (length only). A record for each row of the array is automatically added to the datafile.

Valid *<file-types>* are dBASEII, DELIMITED, DELIMITED WITH BLANK, DELIMITED WITH *<character>*, DIF (VisiCalc), FW2, FW3, and FW4 (Framework II, III and IV), RPD (RapidFile), SDF (System Data Format ASCII file), SYLK (MultiPlan), and WKS (Lotus 1-2-3).

Blank rows in any spreadsheet file type are converted to blank records for the datafile.

APPEND MEMO

Purpose

Reads a file into the specified memo field of the open database.

Command Syntax

APPEND MEMO <*memo-field-name*> **FROM** <*file-name*> [OVERWRITE]

From the dot prompt

Include the OVERWRITE clause to replace the existing memo field data; otherwise, the new information is appended to the existing memo data.

From the Control Center

1. Position the bounce bar on a field and press **Enter** to select it.
2. When asked, select the Display Data option.
3. From the Records menu, select Add New Records.
4. Position the cursor in the memo field marker, and then press **Ctrl-Home** to open the memo field.
5. Press **F10** to access the menu and select Words/Write/Read Text File/Read Text from the File.

Notes

The database must include a memo field before you issue this command.

An error occurs if you specify a field that does not exist or is not a memo field.

ASSIST

Purpose

Accesses the dBASE IV Control Center screen rather than the dot prompt.

Command Syntax

ASSIST

From the dot prompt

1. Type **ASSIST** or press **F2**.
2. Return to the dot prompt from the Control Center screen by pressing **Esc** and answer Yes to end the current operation.

Note

Begin every session at the Control Center by changing the CONFIG.DB file. It must include the COMMAND=ASSIST command line. (This is a default line in the CONFIG.DB file when installed.)

AVERAGE

See *CALCULATE*.

BEGIN/END TRANS

Purpose

Records changes to a database with the option to return back to the original state of the database.

Command Syntax

BEGIN TRANSACTION [<*path-name*>]
<*commands*>

END TRANSACTION

ROLLBACK [<*datafile-name*>]

From the dot prompt

Use the ROLLBACK command to restore the database file to its pretransaction state.

Notes

The ROLLBACK command is effective for the APPEND, BROWSE, CHANGE, DELETE, EDIT, RECALL, REPLACE, and UPDATE commands. Also, create new files by using the COPY, CREATE, IMPORT FROM, INDEX, JOIN, SET CATALOG, SORT, and TOTAL commands.

If you intend to use the rollback capability, you cannot close or overwrite any open files.

Each BEGIN TRANSACTION command line must have a matching END TRANSACTION command line.

The RESET command line tags the files involved in transaction processing. It marks the file when processing begins and is removed upon completion of the procedure or when the ROLLBACK command is used.

Do not include the CLEAR ALL, CLOSE, DELETE FILE, ERASE, INSERT, MODIFY STRUCTURE, PACK, RENAME or ZAP commands in transaction processing.

BLANK

Purpose

Fills records or fields with blanks.

Command Syntax

BLANK [FIELDS <*field-list*>/LIKE/EXCEPT <*skeleton*>] [REINDEX] [<*scope*>] [FOR <*condition*>] [WHILE <*condition*>]

From the dot prompt

1. Issue the **BLANK** command from the dot prompt or from within a program.
2. Optionally specify a condition to select records to be blanked, or select fields to be blanked. The REINDEX option can be used to rebuild indexes after records have been blanked.

From the Control Center

In the Edit or Browse screens, select Blank record from the Records menu to blank the current record.

Note

Fields that have been designated as read-only cannot be blanked.

BROWSE

Purpose

Allows viewing/changing the information in an existing datafile and is used to control modification of data.

Reminder

You can use the following keys while using the Browse Mode:

Key(s)	Function
Ctrl-U	Flags or unflags a record for deletion.
Ctrl-Q or Esc	Ends the edit session without saving the data changes.
Ctrl-W or Ctrl-End	Ends the edit session and saves the data changes.
PgUp	Moves to the previous screen.
PgDn	Moves to the next screen.
↑	Moves to the previous record.
↓	Moves to the next record.
→	Moves to the next character.
←	Moves to the previous character.
Ctrl-←	Moves to the next field.
Ctrl-→	Moves to the previous field.

Command Syntax

BROWSE [NOINIT] [NOFOLLOW] [NOAPPEND] [NOMENU] [NOEDIT] [NODELETE] [NOCLEAR] [NOORGANIZE] [COMPRESS] [FORMAT] [LOCK *<expN>*] [WIDTH *<expN>*] [FREEZE *<field-name>*] [WINDOW *<window-name>*] [FIELDS *<field-name-1>* [/R] [/*<column-width>*] /*<calculated-field-name-1>*=*<expression-1>* [,*<field-name-2>* [/R] [/*<column-width>*] /*<calculated-field-2>* = *<expression-2>*]...]

From the dot prompt

1. Open the file with the **USE** command.
2. Type **BROWSE**, select any desired options, and press **Enter**.
3. View and change any information in the database. Press **Ctrl-End** to save the changes and return to the dot prompt.
4. Close the open database by typing **USE** and pressing **Enter**.

From the Control Center

1. Position the bounce bar on the datafile name.
2. Press **F2**. The Browse Mode is available on-screen.
3. Press **F10** and select the Exit option from the Exit submenu.

Notes

Press **F10** and select the Go To submenu to move the cursor to the top, bottom, or record number within the field. Also, use the submenu to search the file in the specified field for a specified value.

Include the NOAPPEND clause to prevent the user from adding new records. Attempted changes cause the computer to beep.

Pressing Esc or Ctrl-Q after making changes in the Browse screen does not save the changes to the file on disk. The datafile must be closed before you end the dBASE IV session.

CALCULATE

Purpose

Performs math with all or selected records in the open datafile.

Command Syntax

CALCULATE [*<scope>*]*<option-list>* [FOR *<condition>*] [WHILE *<condition>*] [TO *<memvar-list>*/TO ARRAY *<array-name>*]

AVERAGE [*expN-list*] [*<scope>*] [FOR*<condition>*] [WHILE*<condition>*] [TO *<memvar-list>*/TO ARRAY *<array-name>*]

COUNT [TO *<memvar>*] [*<scope>*] [FOR *<condition>*] [WHILE *<condition>*]

SUM [*expN-list>*] [TO *<memvar-list>*/TO ARRAY *<array-name>*] [*<scope>*] [FOR *<condition>*] [WHILE *<condition>*]

From the dot prompt

1. Open the datafile.
2. Display the sum of a numeric field in the open datafile.
3. Display the average of a numeric field.

4. Close the open datafile with the USE or CLOSE command before ending the dBASE IV session.

From the Control Center

1. Press ↓ to position the bounce bar on a field. Press **Enter** twice to open the datafile.
2. Press → to move the bounce bar to the Create option. Press **Enter** to move to a query screen for the datafile. The set of boxes at the bottom identifies the fields included in the query. This is called the View. All database fields are included in the View when you begin a query.
3. Position the bounce bar in a numeric column and type **MIN**. Press **F2** to query the datafile for the record with the smallest number in that field.
4. Press **Esc** to exit the View. When asked if you want to save the query, select the No option and return to the Control Center.

Note

Queries do not change the original datafile; they create a temporary file.

CALL

Purpose

Performs special tasks by running binary programs that are written in a programming language other than dBASE IV.

Command Syntax

CALL <*module-name*> [WITH <*expression-list*>]

From the dot prompt

1. Use the **LOAD** command to read the binary program from the disk.
2. Use the **CALL** command line to run the binary program.
3. When the program ends, issue the **RELEASE MODULE** command to remove the binary program from computer memory.

Notes

The non-dBASE IV program must be loaded with the LOAD command before it can be run with the CALL command.

The program must be read from disk into memory with the LOAD command. Run the program by issuing a **CALL** command. Then remove it from memory with the **RELEASE MODULE** command.

When it is no longer needed, always remove the loaded program from computer memory. Otherwise, you may experience an `Insufficient Memory` error while running an application.

CANCEL

Purpose

Stops a program and closes all open programs. The dot prompt returns immediately.

Command Syntax

CANCEL

From the dot prompt

1. Include the CANCEL command in a program to cancel the program and return control to the dot prompt or Control Center.
2. Place the CANCEL command within an IF, ENDIF or DO CASE, ENDCASE command set to allow conditional execution of the CANCEL command; or press Esc after typing in a single command. When asked Cancel, Suspend, or Ignore, select Cancel to return to the dot prompt.

From the Control Center

Press Esc to stop the processing of a query, report, or program. When asked Cancel, Suspend, or Ignore, select Cancel to return to the Control Center.

Notes

This command does not close the open files of a database.

All private memory variables are released before control returns to the dot prompt or Control Center. To save private variables, use SUSPEND rather than CANCEL.

Use the CANCEL command to stop processing the application. The user is returned to the dot prompt or Control Center.

Use the RETURN command in programs when you want to go back to the program (or dot prompt) that initiated the program containing the RETURN command.

Caution

Enclose each of these commands within an IF, ENDIF or DO CASE, ENDCASE command set. Otherwise, the CANCEL is encountered immediately.

CHANGE

See *EDIT*.

CLEAR

Purpose

Removes information from the screen or computer memory.

Command Syntax

CLEAR [ALL/FIELDS/GETS/MEMORY/MENUS/
POPUPS/SCREENS/TYPEAHEAD/WINDOWS]

From the dot prompt

1. Include the **ALL** clause to close open datafiles and to release all memory variables, arrays, pop-ups, and menu definitions. Issuing the CLEAR ALL command is like starting a new dBASE IV session.

2. To remove information selectively, use the appropriate clause.

Notes

The CLEAR command causes dBASE IV to remove the specified information.

Using the CLEAR command without any of the options only clears the screen. All information remains in memory.

If a memory variable used by a program is removed accidentally, it causes a `Variable not found` error.

CLOSE

Purpose

Closes an open datafile in a work area and saves all changes. Also closes Alternate, Format, Index and Procedure files.

Reminder

Issue the USE or CLOSE commands to close open datafiles.

Command Syntax

CLOSE ALL/ALTERNATE/DATABASES/FORMAT/
INDEXES/PROCEDURE/PRINTER

From the dot prompt

1. Open at least one datafile with the USE command.
2. Read, change, or report on information in the datafile.
3. Use CLOSE DATABASES to close all open datafiles.

From the Control Center

1. Position the bounce bar on a datafile name in the Data column.
2. Perform your work with the open datafile.
3. Position the bounce bar on the file and press Enter twice to close the selected datafile.

COMPILE

Purpose

Changes a program from readable source code to object code.

Command Syntax

COMPILE <*file-name*> [RUNTIME]

From the dot prompt

Save the new or changed program on disk. When the dot prompt returns, use the COMPILE command to initiate the compiler.

From the Control Center

Select Save and run the program from the Exit submenu. If the program was changed, the date and time stamp on the source file differs from the object file and dBASE IV automatically recompiles the program.

Notes

Use the SET DEVELOPMENT command to turn on or off automatic program compilation.

Before dBASE IV runs a program, it checks the date and time stamp of the .PRG (source) file against the .DBO (object) file. If they do not agree, the source program must be recompiled to utilize the most recent changes.

Caution

Each command line in the program is checked for proper syntax during the compilation process. If an error is encountered, a message and the line number on which the error occurred appear on-screen. Errors abort the program compilation process.

CONTINUE

See *LOCATE*.

CONVERT

Purpose

Changes the structure of a single-user datafile by adding a new field for multiuser access.

Reminder

After the datafile is converted to be multiuser, it need not be converted again. The _dbaselock stores the following values:

Count	A 2-byte hexadecimal number used to record the number of times the record is changed.
Time	A 3-byte hexadecimal number that records the time a lock occurred.
Date	A 3-byte hexadecimal number that records the date a lock occurred.
Name	The log-in name of the user that locked the record.

Command Syntax

CONVERT [TO <*expN*>]

From the dot prompt

1. Use the **CONVERT** command to insert a character field called _dbaselock in the datafile structure.
2. Write a program to prompt for a customer number.
3. Use **SEEK** or **FIND** to locate the proper record. If it is found, allow record modification. dBASE IV records the count, time, date, and user in the _dbaselock field.
4. When changes are completed, issue an **UNLOCK** command to release the record to other users.

COPY

Purpose

Makes a duplicate of all, or a selected set, of records from the datafile.

Reminder

Use a **COPY** command or a query to create datafiles that include only the information that you need for your work.

Command Syntax

COPY TO <*file-name*> [[TYPE] <*file-type*>]/ [[WITH] PRODUCTION] [FIELDS <*field-list*>] [<*scope*>] [FOR <*condition*>] [WHILE <*condition*>]

COPY STRUCTURE TO *<file-name>* [FIELDS *<field-list>*] [[WITH] PRODUCTION]

COPY TO *<file-name>* **STRUCTURE EXTENDED**

COPY TO ARRAY *<array-name>* [FIELDS *<field-list>*] [*<scope>*] [FOR *<condition>*] [WHILE *<condition>*]

COPY FILE *<file-name>* **TO** *<file-name>*

COPY INDEXES *<index-file-list>* [TO *<multiple-index>*]

COPY MEMO *<memo-field-name>* **TO** *<file-name>* [ADDITIVE]

COPY TAG *<tag-name>* [OF *<multiple-file-name>*] **TO** *<index-file-name>*

From the dot prompt

1. Open one of the datafiles with the **USE** command.
2. Issue the **COPY TO** command to create a file from the open one.
3. Close the open datafile.

From the Control Center

1. Open the datafile.
2. Use a query to create a new datafile of selected records.
3. Use the Catalog submenu to create a duplicate of a file.

Notes

An array must be established with the **DECLARE** command. Then use the **COPY TO ARRAY** command to hold data from at least one record from the open datafile. Refer to each item by its subscript.

The REPLACE FROM ARRAY command is used to restore values to a database from an array.

COUNT

See *CALCULATE.*

CREATE APPLICATION

Purpose

Designs and uses the dBASE IV Applications Generator to write programs.

Command Syntax

CREATE/MODIFY APPLICATION *<file-name>* **/?**

From the dot prompt

1. Issue **CREATE APPLICATION** to access the Applications Generator.
2. A window opens and input areas are available for the Application name, Description, Main menu type and name, Database/View, and Index/Order information. If you use multiple index files, you must specify the main index in the ORDER input area.
3. When all input areas are correct, press **Ctrl-End**.

4. Supply information for the sign-on screen.
5. Open the menu and select Application/Generate Quick Application.
6. A window opens. Fill in the data, screen format, report format, label format, index files, and main menu names. Press **Ctrl-End** when all input areas are correct. Press a key when prompted.
7. Select Yes to generate the application.
8. Position the bounce bar on the Save Current Application Definition option to save the application on disk.
9. Exit from the Applications Generator.
10. Issue a **DO** command to see the results of your work.

From the Control Center

1. Select the Create option in the Applications column. When prompted, type **A** to select the Applications Generator.
2. Create the application by following the dot prompt procedure, steps 2 through 9.
3. Run the application by selecting the option from the Applications column of the Control Center screen.

CREATE FROM

Purpose

Creates a new dBASE IV datafile from another datafile.

Command Syntax

CREATE *<file-name>* **FROM** *<extended-structure-file>*

From the dot prompt

1. Use the **CREATE FROM** command to specify the name of the datafile to be created from the datafile that contains the field information.
2. When the dot prompt returns, the new datafile is available on the disk.

CREATE/MODIFY LABEL

Purpose

Designs and prints labels for an open datafile.

Command Syntax

CREATE/MODIFY LABEL *<file-name>* **/?**

From the dot prompt

1. Issue the **CREATE LABEL** command to design a new screen format.
2. Press **F10** to access the menu line at the top of the screen.
3. From the Dimensions submenu, select Predefined Size and a label type. Press **Enter**.
4. Open the Fields submenu and select Add Field to select field names.
5. Select the fields for your labels. When asked for template information, press **Ctrl-End**.

6. Open the Layout submenu and select Save This Label Design.
7. When prompted, supply a name for the label format.
8. Open the Print submenu and select Begin Printing.
9. Open the Exit submenu and select the Save Changes and Exit option to return to the dot prompt.

From the Control Center

1. Open a datafile by pressing **Enter** twice in the data column.
2. Select the Create option in the Labels column.
3. Follow the dot prompt procedure (steps 2 through 9) to create and save the label format.

Note

Use the print submenu to control printing options.

CREATE/MODIFY QUERY/VIEW

Purpose

Extracts records from datafiles.

Reminder

If the specified query file does not exist on the disk, the MODIFY QUERY command lets you create it.

Command Syntax

CREATE/MODIFY QUERY *<file-name>*/?

CREATE/MODIFY VIEW *<file-name>*/?

From the dot prompt

1. Include the ? clause to open a window of existing query files.
2. Select a query from the list.

From the Control Center

1. Open a datafile. Press → to select the Create option in the queries column.
2. Press **F10** and select Add File to Query. Select a second datafile. Move the highlighted input area to the key field in a datafile.
3. Select the Create Link by Pointing option.
4. Press **F3** (up) or **F4** (down) to move to the other file layout. Place the input area where LINK1 appears in the field column.
5. Press **F5** to add fields from the new datafile to the view.
6. Complete the query definition, press **F10**, and then select Save This Query. Type the query name in the input area.
7. Press **F2** to begin the search of the data.

Note

Do not exceed 20 calculations per query screen.

CREATE/MODIFY REPORT

Purpose

Designs and uses report forms to print records from the open datafile(s). Prints columnar reports, special forms, and Mailmerge documents.

Command Syntax

CREATE/MODIFY REPORT *<file-name>*/?

From the dot prompt

1. Issue the **CREATE REPORT** command to design a new datafile screen format.
2. Press **F10**, select the layout, and select the Quick Layouts option.
3. Select Column Layout. A columnar report format with all fields in the datafile appears. The field name is the column heading.
4. Press **F10** and use the menus to customize your report. When you are finished, select Layout/Save This Report, supply a name, and press **Enter**.
5. Use the **MODIFY REPORT** command to change an existing screen file format.
6. When a report form exists, use the **REPORT FORM** command to send the report to the screen. Add the **TO PRINT** option to send the report to a printer.

From the Control Center

1. Open the datafile. Select the Create option in the Reports column.

2. Select Quick Layouts from the Layout menu.
3. Follow the dot prompt procedure to change the form (steps 3 and 4).
4. From the Control Center screen, select the file name from the Reports column.
5. When prompted, select Print report. The report is sent to the printer.

Notes

Select the Form Layout option when you need to provide one record per page.

Use the Box option from the Layout submenu to print a box on the report page.

An 8 1/2-by-11-inch sheet of paper accommodates 80 positions in the normal print font or 132 positions in condensed print. An 11-by-14-inch sheet of paper accommodates 132 positions in normal print or 210 positions in condensed print.

CREATE/MODIFY SCREEN

Purpose

Designs and saves record maintenance screens that include meaningful labels. Used rather than the Browse screen.

Command Syntax

CREATE/MODIFY SCREEN *<file-name>*/?

From the dot prompt

1. Type USE and the name of the database for which you want to design a screen format.

2. Use **CREATE** or **MODIFY SCREEN** to design or change a datafile screen format.
3. Press **F10** to access the menu line at the top of the screen.
4. Select Quick Layout to create a new screen format.
5. Use the submenus to change the screen format.
6. Save the screen format by selecting Save Changes and Exit.

From the Control Center

1. Open the datafile.
2. Select Create from the Forms column.
3. Create and save the screen format for the open datafile, as shown in dot prompt procedure (steps 3 through 5).
4. From the Control Center, select the file name from the Forms column.

Notes

To move an area on the screen format, press **F6**, the arrow keys, and **Enter** to specify the entire area and its contents. Then press **F7**, the arrow keys, and **Enter** to move the selected area to another part of the screen.

Unless you specify that you want to use the screen format, the Browse or Append screens are used.

CREATE or MODIFY STRUCTURE

Purpose

Creates or changes a layout for a dBASE IV datafile.

Command Syntax

CREATE *<file-name>*

MODIFY STRUCTURE

From the dot prompt

1. Type **CREATE** and a file name to create a new datafile. A blank structure appears for field information.
2. Type the name, type, and length for each field you want to keep in the datafile. Press **Ctrl-End** to return to the dot prompt and keep the new structure.
3. Change the datafile structure at any time. First, open the datafile with the **USE** command. Then issue the **MODIFY STRUCTURE** command.

From the Control Center

1. Select the Create option in the Data column. A datafile structure input form is presented on-screen.
2. Type the information for each field in the input areas.
3. Press **Ctrl-N** to insert a new field or **Ctrl-U** to delete a field.

4. Press **Enter** or **Ctrl-End** to return to the Control Center. When prompted, type a file name for the new file.

5. Press **N** or **Y** when asked whether you want to input data.

Caution

Do not change field names at the same time you insert or delete fields. Also, do not change a field name at the same time you change the width or type.

DEACTIVATE MENU

See *DEFINE MENU/DEFINE PAD*.

DEACTIVATE POPUP

See *DEFINE POPUP*.

DEACTIVATE WINDOW

See *DEFINE WINDOW*.

DEBUG

Purpose

Tests new or changed dBASE IV programs.

Command Syntax

DEBUG *<file-name>*/*<procedure-name>* [**WITH** *<parameter-list>*]

From the dot prompt

1. Use the **DEBUG** command to run the program or procedure. The box in the upper left corner displays the program. The highlighted bar identifies the next command to be performed.
2. The box at the top right is the command box. Use it as a reference to specify the next action.
3. Use the DISPLAY box to specify fields, variables, and arrays. The DEBUGGER window displays information about the datafile, procedure, and program as you step through the program.

Note

Include the **SUSPEND** command in a program to stop the program temporarily. Use **RESUME** to continue running the program.

DECLARE

Purpose

Establishes an array. This command specifies the name, length, and width of the array.

Command Syntax

DECLARE *<array-name-1>* [{*<number-of-rows>*,} *<number-of-columns>*] {,*<array-name-2>* [{*<number-of-rows>*,} *<number-of-columns>*]...}

From the dot prompt

1. Issue the **DECLARE** command from the dot prompt or in a program to create an array.
2. Set the value of the elements with the **=** or **STORE** command.

Notes

Use subscripts to address the array elements.

Use the **DISPLAY MEMORY** or **?** command to display the values in the array.

DEFINE BAR

See *DEFINE POPUP*.

DEFINE BOX

Purpose

Defines boxes for reports.

Command Syntax

DEFINE BOX FROM *<print-column>* **TO** *<print-column>* HEIGHT *<expN>* [AT LINE *<print-line>*] [SINGLE/DOUBLE/*<border-definition-string>*]

From the dot prompt

1. Issue the DEFINE BOX command from the dot prompt or in a program. Specify the line number, column number, and character to be used for the border.
2. Set the _box memory variable to True when you want to print the box. When the print advances past the lines specified in the DEFINE BOX command, the box is printed on the page.

From the Control Center

Select the Box option from the Layout submenu when creating a report format.

DEFINE MENU, DEFINE PAD

Purpose

Builds bounce bar menus.

Command Syntax

DEFINE MENU *<menu-name>* [MESSAGE *<expC>*]

DEFINE PAD *<pad-name>* OF *<menu-name>*
PROMPT *<expC>* [AT *<row>*,*<col>*]
[MESSAGE*<expC>*]

ACTIVATE MENU *<menu-name>* [PAD *<pad-name>*]

DEACTIVATE MENU

ON SELECTION PAD *<pad-name>* OF *<menu-name>*
[*<command>*]

SHOW MENU *<menu-name>* [PAD *<pad-name>*]

From the dot prompt

1. Use **DEFINE MENU** to begin the menu command set and assign it a name. Each DEFINE PAD command line identifies a menu option. It also provides an option name, a prompt, and screen positioning.

   Each DEFINE PAD command should have an ON SELECTION PAD command as shown:

   ```
   ON SELECTION PAD MAINT of MENU1
      DO MAINT ON SELECTION PAD
      REPORTS OF MENU1 DO PRTRPTS
   ```

2. Activate the menu by typing **ACTIVATE MENU MENU1**.

3. When finished with a menu, use the **DEACTIVATE MENU** command.

From the Control Center

When you create an application through the Application column of the Control Center, you can use a bar menu or a pop-up menu.

Notes

Combine the **DEFINE MENU**, **DEFINE PAD**, and **ACTIVATE MENU** commands to create the menu.

Use the **ACTIVATE MENU** command to provide a menu to the user. The DEACTIVATE MENU command erases the menu from the screen but not memory.

Include the **RELEASE POPUP** command in the program to remove the menu definition from memory. Otherwise, you may experience an `Insufficient Memory` error while running an application.

DEFINE POPUP

Purpose

Provides a window that contains specific information, messages, and a border.

Command Syntax

DEFINE POPUP <*popup-name*>

FROM <*row-1*>,<*col-1*> [TO <*row-2*>,<*col-2*>]
[PROMPT FIELD <*field-name*>/

PROMPT FILES [LIKE <*skeleton*>]/PROMPT
STRUCTURE] [MESSAGE <*expC*>]

ACTIVATE POPUP <*popup-name*>

DEACTIVATE POPUP

DEFINE BAR <*line-number*> **OF** <*popup-name*>
PROMPT <*expC*> [MESSAGE <*expC*>] [SKIP
[FOR <*condition*>]]

ON SELECTION POPUP <*popup-name*>**/ALL**
[<*command*>]

SHOW POPUP <*popup-name*>

From the dot prompt

1. Use **DEFINE POPUP** to begin a pop-up definition.
2. Include **PROMPT FIELD** to identify the field values for a datafile.
3. Include **PROMPT FILES** to open a window with a directory listing. Each DEFINE BAR command line identifies a submenu option. The line number, pop-up name, and user prompt are also included.

From the Control Center

When you create an application through the Application column of the Control Center, choose between a bar menu or a pop-up menu.

Notes

Combine the DEFINE POPUP, DEFINE BAR, and ACTIVATE POPUP commands to create the submenu.

Use the ACTIVATE POPUP command to provide a pop-up to the user. The DEACTIVATE POPUP command erases the pop-up from the screen but not from memory.

The SHOW POPUP command displays the specified pop-up menu on-screen; however, the menu is not available to the user.

Include an ON SELECTION POPUP command for each option to identify the action to be taken when the user selects the option.

Include the RELEASE POPUP command in the program to remove the pop-up definition from memory. Otherwise, you may experience an `Insufficient Memory` error while running an application.

DEFINE WINDOW

Purpose

Provides a defined area of information on-screen for the user. Enables you to define borders and colors of screen windows.

Command Syntax

DEFINE WINDOW *<window-name>* **FROM** *<row-1>*,*<col-1>* TO *<row-2>*,*<col-2>* [DOUBLE/PANEL/NONE/*<border-definition-string>*] [COLOR [*<standard>*] [,*<enhanced>*] [,*<frame>*]]

ACTIVATE WINDOW *<window-name-list>*/**ALL**

DEACTIVATE WINDOW *<window-name-list>*/**ALL**

MOVE WINDOW *<window-name>* **TO** *<row>*,*<column>*/**BY** *<delta-row>*,*<delta-column>*

From the dot prompt

1. Use the **DEFINE WINDOW** command to draw a box on-screen. Specify a name, an area, a type, and colors for the box.
2. Provide the name of the defined window in the ACTIVATE WINDOW command line when you want to display it on-screen.
3. Issue the **MOVE WINDOW** command to move the window absolutely (TO) or relatively (BY).
4. Issue a **DEACTIVATE WINDOW** command to remove the window from the screen. The information overlaid returns to the screen for the user.

From the Control Center

When you create an application through the Application column of the Control Center, you may define a window as in the DOT PROMPT.

Notes

Include the **RELEASE WINDOW** command in the program to remove window definitions from memory. Otherwise, you may experience an `Insufficient Memory` error while running an application.

DELETE

Purpose

Flags records for removal from the open datafile.

Command Syntax

DELETE [<*scope*>] [FOR <*condition*>] [WHILE <*condition*>]

PACK

From the dot prompt

1. Open a datafile. Use the **GO** command to move to the record you want removed from the datafile.
2. Display the record to make sure that it is the correct record.
3. Type **DELETE** and press **Enter**.
4. Display the record again. The asterisk marks or identifies this record for removal from the datafile.
5. Type **PACK** and press **Enter** to remove the marked record.

From the Control Center

1. Open a datafile and press **F2** to use the Browse screen.
2. Use the arrow keys to move to the record you want to remove from the datafile.
3. Press **F10** and press ↓ to position the bounce bar to Mark Record for Deletion, and then press **Enter**.

4. Press **F10** again. Use Clear Deletion Mark to remove the deletion flag.
5. Select the Exit option from the Exit submenu to return to the Control Center.

Note

Limit the effect of the DELETE and RECALL commands by specifying a condition.

DELETE FILE

See *ERASE*.

DELETE TAG

Purpose

Removes a tag from a multiple index file.

Command Syntax

DELETE TAG <*tag-name-1*> [OF <*multiple-index-file-name*>] [,<*tag-name-2*> [OF <*multiple-index-file-name*>] ...]

From the dot prompt

Issue a **DELETE TAG** command to remove a tag name from a multiple index file.

From the Control Center

From the Modify Structure screen, select the Remove Unwanted Index Tag option from the Organize submenu to remove tags from the multiple index file. You also can reach the Organize menu from the Browse screen.

Notes

A multiple index file contains a maximum of 47 tags (sort orders).

Include multiple tag names in a DELETE TAG command.

Specify a proper tag name in the DELETE TAG command line so that dBASE IV does not report an error.

DEXPORT

Purpose

Creates a Binary Named List (BNL) file from a screen, report, or label design file.

Command Syntax

DEXPORT SCREEN/REPORT/LABEL <*file-name*> [TO <*BNL-file-name*>]

From the dot prompt

Issue the DEXPORT command from the dot prompt or from within a program and specify the type of file you want to create.

Note

dBASE IV uses the following file extensions for BNL files:

File	Extension
Screens	.SNL
Reports	.FNL
Labels	.LNL

DIR

Purpose

Performs a directory operation that is available from the dot prompt.

Command Syntax

DIRECTORY/DIR [[ON] <*drive*>:] [[LIKE] [<*path*>] <*skeleton*>]

From the dot prompt

Use the DIR command to list files on the current disk. Issue the DIR command without any of the options to list only the datafiles (.DBF).

From the Control Center

1. Press **F10** to access the menu line at the top of the screen.
2. Select the Tools/DOS Utilities options. A window that contains file names, lengths, date, time, attributes, and space used appears on-screen. Press **F10** to use the submenu options included on-screen.
3. Use the Files submenu to change the drive or subdirectory or to specify the type of files you want to appear in the DOS directory window of the Control Center.

Note

A DIR command without a skeleton lists only the .DBF files on the disk.

DISPLAY

See *LIST*.

DO

Purpose

Runs dBASE IV programs.

Command Syntax

DO *<program-name>*/*<procedure-name>* [WITH *<parameter-list>*]

From the dot prompt

Run the program by issuing the **DO** command. If the program has changed since the last compilation, dBASE IV evaluates it for errors.

From the Control Center

1. Position the bounce bar on the selected option in the Application column and press **Enter**.
2. When prompted, select Run Application.

DO CASE, ENDCASE

Purpose

Controls program flow based on data values.

Command Syntax

DO CASE
[CASE *<condition-1>* *<commands-1>*] [CASE *<condition-2>* *<commands>*] [OTHERWISE *<commands>*]

ENDCASE

From the dot prompt

1. Use the **DO CASE**, **ENDCASE** command set to mark the beginning and end of a conditional situation. Each CASE command within the set is evaluated until a condition is met, or all conditions are false.
2. When one of the CASE conditions is evaluated as true, the command lines that follow it are processed and all other CASE lines are

skipped. If no cases are found true, the commands after OTHERWISE are processed. Processing continues with the lines that follow the ENDCASE command.

From the Control Center

Follow the steps from the dot prompt when generating applications.

Notes

The effect of this command set is the same as the IF, ENDIF command set.

Include the OTHERWISE clause in the DO CASE, ENDCASE command set when you want to supply command lines for a situation that does not meet any of the CASE conditions.

DO WHILE, ENDDO

Purpose

Performs a set of command lines until some condition is met.

Command Syntax

DO WHILE *<condition>*
  <commands>
  [LOOP]
  [EXIT]

ENDDO

From the dot prompt

Use DO WHILE <*condition*> and ENDDO to establish a set of command lines you want to perform until a condition is met.

From the Control Center

Looping is done automatically when you use selections from the Queries, Forms, Reports, and Labels columns of the Control Center.

Notes

The effect of this command set is the same as the SCAN, ENDSCAN command set. However, when processing a datafile, include the SKIP command to move the record pointer. The record pointer movement is not handled automatically.

Include the LOOP command within the loop in the program to force dBASE IV to reevaluate a condition. When the LOOP command is encountered, the command lines following the loop are ignored and the condition is reviewed. If the condition is still true, the loop continues.

Use EXIT to end the looping activity immediately. When this command is encountered, the program continues running with the command following the ENDDO line.

EDIT

Purpose

Changes the information in an existing datafile.

Command Syntax

EDIT [NOINIT] [NOFOLLOW] [NOAPPEND] [NOMENU] [NOEDIT] [NODELETE] [NOCLEAR] [NOORGANIZE] [<*record-number*>] [FIELDS <*field-list*>] [<*scope*>] [FOR <*condition*>] [WHILE <*condition*>]

CHANGE [NOINIT] [NOFOLLOW] [NOAPPEND] [NOMENU] [NOEDIT] [NODELETE] [NOCLEAR] [NOORGANIZE] [<*record-number*>] [FIELDS <*field-list*>] [<*scope*>] [FOR <*condition*>] [WHILE <*condition*>]

From the dot prompt

1. Open the datafile. Use **GOTO**, **LOCATE**, **FIND**, or **SEEK** to move the record pointer to the record you want.
2. Type **EDIT** and press **Enter** to change each field of the record.
3. Change the information. Then press **Ctrl-End** to save the changes and return to the dot prompt.

From the Control Center

1. Position the bounce bar on the datafile name.
2. Press **F2**. Use the Browse screen to edit the data.

Notes

You can use the following keys while editing data:

Key(s)	Description
Ctrl-U	Flags or unflags a record for deletion.
Esc	Ends the edit session without saving data changes.

Ctrl-End	Ends the edit session and saves the data changes.
PgUp	Moves to the previous screen.
PgDn	Moves to the next screen.
↑	Moves to the previous field or record.
↓	Moves to the next field or record.
→	Moves to the next character.
←	Moves to the previous character.

Include the **NOINIT**, **NOFOLLOW**, **NOAPPEND**, **NOMENU**, **NOORGANIZE**, **NOEDIT**, **NODELETE**, and **NOCLEAR** clauses to control the edit activity.

Replace the *<record-number>* with a valid record number. Include the **FIELDS** *<field-list>* clause to specify the fields to be presented on-screen. The *<scope>*, FOR *<condition>*, and WHILE *<condition>* clauses specify a range of datafile records.

Pressing **Esc** or **Ctrl-Q** after making changes does not save the changes to the file on disk. The datafile must be closed before you end the dBASE IV session.

EJECT, EJECT PAGE

Purpose

Moves the paper in the printer to the top of the next page.

Command Syntax

EJECT

EJECT PAGE

From the dot prompt

1. Issue an EJECT command. The paper moves to the top of the next page.
2. When the EJECT PAGE command is encountered, the headers and footers specified by the ON PAGE command line are printed as the printer advances to the next page.

From the Control Center

1. When you select a report from the Reports or Labels column, you are asked whether you want to print the information. Answer Yes.
2. A window of print options opens on-screen. Select the Eject Page Now option before or after selecting the Begin Printing option.

Note

Use the SET DEVICE TO or SET PRINT commands to turn the printer on and off for @...SAY, ?, or ?? commands.

ERASE

Purpose

Removes a file from the disk without ending the dBASE IV session.

Command Syntax

ERASE *<file-name>*/?

DELETE FILE *<file-name>*/?

From the dot prompt

Issue a **DELETE FILE** or **ERASE** command from the prompt or within a program to remove the specified file from the disk.

From the Control Center

1. Press **F10** to access the menu line at the top of the screen.
2. Select the Tools/DOS Utilities options. A window that contains file names, file size, date, time, attributes, and space used appears on-screen.
3. Move the selection bar to the file(s) you desire to delete. Press **Enter** to mark each file.
4. Use the Operations menu to delete the marked file(s).
5. Use the Exit menu to return to the Control Center screen.

EXPORT

Purpose

Sends dBASE IV data to other popular software packages.

Reminder

You can export dBASE IV data to RapidFile, dBASE II, Lotus 1-2-3, PFS:File, or Framework versions II, III and IV.

Command Syntax

EXPORT TO <*file-name*> [TYPE] **RPD/DBASEII/WK1/WKS/PFS/FW2/FW3/FW4** [FIELDS <*field-list*>] [<*scope*>] [FOR <*condition*>] [WHILE <*condition*>]

From the dot prompt

1. Open the dBASE IV datafile that contains the data to export.
2. At the next dot prompt, type **EXPORT TO C:\FW\SALES.FW2 TYPE FW2** to export a dBASE IV file to a Framework II file in the FW subdirectory on drive C.
3. Type **USE** to close the datafile.

From the Control Center

1. Open the datafile to be used to create the new file.
2. Press **F10**, open the Tools submenu, and select the Export option. A window of file types appears on-screen.
3. Use the arrow keys to position the bounce bar on the type of file being created from the dBASE IV datafile. Press **Enter** to select it.
4. Type the name of the file and press **Enter** to start the transfer.

FIND

Purpose

Looks through the data in the open field for specific information that matches the key fields used to index it.

Command Syntax

FIND *<literal-key>*

From the dot prompt

1. Open the database file specifying the index key.
2. To search for a value in the key field, type **FIND** followed by the value sought.

   If the record is not located, the message `Record not found` appears.
3. If the record is found and you want to find another record that matches your search criterion, type **CONTINUE** and press **Enter**.
4. Close the open datafile by typing **USE** and pressing **Enter**.

From the Control Center

1. Highlight the datafile you want to use, press **Enter**, and select Display Data.

   Press **Enter** to move the bounce bar to the field you want to search.
2. Press **F10** to access the menu at the top of the screen. Open the Go To submenu and select the Index Key Search option.

3. When asked for the search string, type it in the input area and press **Enter**. If it is not found, the computer beeps and tells you that the value was not found in the datafile.
4. Press **Esc** to return to the Go To submenu. Otherwise, the submenus are removed and the bounce bar is positioned on the requested record.
5. To return to the Control Center, press **Esc** or select the Exit option from the Exit submenu.

Notes

Upper- and lowercase letters must be considered when you are providing search criteria. If the Control Center's Match Capitalization option in the Settings submenu equals Yes, or the dot prompt's SET EXACT command is ON, all character positions must match in case as well as length.

When using a search command in a program, use the FOUND() function in an IF command to determine whether the desired record was found during the search.

FUNCTION

Purpose

A section of a program that performs specialized tasks.

Command Syntax

FUNCTION *<procedure-name>*

From the dot prompt

A function is identified by the FUNCTION command as the first line and the RETURN command as the last line. The RETURN command line must send information back to the calling program or procedure.

Notes

Identify a user-defined function by including the **FUNCTION** command line at the top of the command set. It continues until the RETURN command line is encountered.

Use the **PARAMETER** command line as the first line of a function that expects information from the calling program.

GO, GOTO

Purpose

Moves the record pointer within the datafile.

Command Syntax

GO/GOTO BOTTOM/TOP [IN <*alias*>]

GO/GOTO [RECORD] <*record-number*> [IN <*alias*>]
<*record-number*>

From the dot prompt

1. Open a datafile with the **USE** command.
2. Type **GO 3** and press **Enter**. The name of the datafile and the record number appear on the Status line.

3. Type **DISPLAY** and press **Enter**.

   Record number 3 appears on-screen.

4. Move to the first record in the datafile by typing **GO TOP** and pressing **Enter**. Then display it on-screen.

5. Move the record pointer to the end of the datafile by typing **GO BOTTOM** and pressing **Enter**. Display it on-screen.

From the Control Center

1. Position the cursor on a file name in the Data column. Press **F2** to display the data in a browse screen.

2. Press **F10** to access the menu at the top of the screen. Then open the Go To submenu and select the Last Record option. The last record in the datafile moves to the top of the screen.

3. Access the Go To submenu again. Select the Record Number option. When asked for the record number, type **3** and press **Enter**. Record number 3 moves to the top line of the data screen.

Note

If you go to the bottom of the datafile (GO BOTTOM), and then issue a SKIP command from the dot prompt, an extra record number appears although the record is not there.

HELP

Purpose

Displays instructions or assistance.

Command Syntax

HELP [<*dBASE IV keyword*>]

From the dot prompt

1. Type **HELP** at the dot prompt and press **Enter**. A menu of help options appears on-screen.
2. Press ↑ and ↓ to position the bounce bar on the desired option. Then press **Enter** to open a help window and display information about the selected option.
3. Press **Esc** to return to the dot prompt.

From the Control Center

1. Position the bounce bar on one of the Control Center columns.
2. Press **F1** so that the first help page appears in a window on-screen.
3. Use the arrow keys to position the bounce bar on one of the options at the bottom of the window. Press **Enter** to select it.
4. Press **Esc** to return to the Control Center.

IF, ENDIF

Purpose

Controls the way the data is processed when it meets the specified criteria.

Command Syntax

IF *<condition>* *<true-commands>* [ELSE *<false-commands>*]

ENDIF

From the dot prompt

1. Include the **IF**, **ENDIF** command set to perform one set of commands when the condition is true and, optionally, another set of commands when the condition is false. The IF command line specifies the condition. The commands that follow it (true commands) are performed only when the condition is evaluated as true. Then, processing continues with the commands following the ENDIF.
2. Include the **ELSE** command line when you need command lines that follow it to be performed when the condition is evaluated as false.

From the Control Center

1. Use the query capability to establish the special conditions for a datafile.
2. Set the query and its view so that the data is selected properly. When the report prints, or a datafile is updated, only the data matching the established query will be used. (This only simulates what IF...ENDIF can do.)

Note

An IF always must be used with an ENDIF.

IMPORT

Purpose

Creates dBASE IV files from files used by other popular software packages. Imports data from RapidFile, dBASE II, Lotus 1-2-3, PFS:File, or Framework versions II, III and IV.

Command Syntax

IMPORT FROM *<file-name>* [TYPE] **RPD/DBASEII/ WK1/WKS/PFS/FW2/FW3/FW4**

From the dot prompt

1. At the next dot prompt, type **IMPORT FROM C:\FW\SALES.FW2 TYPE FW2** to import a Framework II file from the FW subdirectory on drive C.
2. Type **USE** to open the new dBASE IV datafile.

From the Control Center

1. Press **F10** to access the menu at the top of the screen. Open the Tools submenu and select the Import option.
2. Use the arrow keys to position the bounce bar on the type of file being imported to dBASE IV and press **Enter** to select it. A window of the selected type of datafiles appears on-screen.
3. Position the bounce bar on the proper file name and press **Enter** to select it.

INDEX

Purpose

Enables you to organize data.

Command Syntax

INDEX ON *<key-expression>* **TO** *<index-file-name>*/ **TAG** *<tag-name>* [OF *<multiple-index-file-name>*] [FOR *<condition>*] [UNIQUE] [DESCENDING]

REINDEX

From the dot prompt

1. Open the datafile.
2. Create an index for the open datafile by using the **INDEX** command.
3. Create a conditional index by using the **FOR** clause to specify a condition that records must meet before being included in the index.

From the Control Center

1. Open a datafile. Press **Shift-F2** to display the data structure and move the bounce bar to the menu line at the top of the screen.
2. The Organize submenu is now active. Position the bounce bar on the Create New Index option and press **Enter** to select it. Another window opens on-screen.
3. Use the options to specify the name of the index, the index expression (key field string), ascending or descending, and whether you want to view duplicate records.

4. Select the Name of Index option. Type the name for the index TAG.
5. Select the Index Expression option and type the fields to be used to organize the data.
6. Press **Ctrl-End**. A window opens and displays the progress of the operation. When it is complete, the datafile structure returns to the screen.

Note

Indexed datafiles only look like they are in the specified order. The records remain in the order that they were entered or sorted.

INPUT

Purpose

Stops the program activity and asks the user for information.

Command Syntax

INPUT [*<prompt>*] **TO** *<memvar>*

From the dot prompt

Type **INPUT "Enter the beginning date" TO MFROM** and press **Enter**. The text within the quotation marks appears on the next line, and the cursor is waiting for you to type a value.

Note

The INPUT command creates character or numeric variables.

INSERT

Purpose

Inserts records in a datafile.

Command Syntax

INSERT [BEFORE] [BLANK] /[NOORGANIZE]

From the dot prompt

1. Open a datafile.
2. Move the record pointer to a record after which you want to insert a new record.
3. Insert a blank record by issuing the **INSERT** command. The screen changes to an APPEND screen for you to type the information into the blank record.

Notes

Include the **BEFORE** clause in the **INSERT** command to put the new record before the current record rather than after it.

If you insert the new record in the wrong place, press **Ctrl-U** or issue the **DELETE** command to flag it for deletion. Then use **PACK**.

JOIN

Purpose

Combines two datafiles.

Command Syntax

JOIN WITH *<alias>* **TO** *<file-name>*

[FIELDS *<field-list>*} FOR *<condition>*

From the dot prompt

Open two datafiles in different areas, and then select the primary datafile and issue the **JOIN** command.

From the Control Center

1. Open the primary datafile. Press → to move the bounce bar to the Create option in the Queries column. Press **Enter** to select it.
2. Press **F10** and select the Add File to Query option from the Layout submenu. When the datafile window opens, select the second datafile for your query.
3. Move the bounce bar to the key field in one of the datafiles.
4. Press **F10** and select the Create Link by Pointing option. When the submenu disappears, LINK1 appears in the selected field.
5. Press **F3** to move up or **F4** to move down to the other file layout. Position the bounce bar in the key field and press **Enter** so that LINK1 appears in the key field column of both query structures.
6. Press **F5** to add or remove fields from each datafile for the view to complete the query definition.
7. Select Write View As Database File from the Layout menu.
8. Specify a file name for the new joined file.

Note

Sort or index the datafiles used in the JOIN operation. The order of the records is important because each command compares key field values.

KEYBOARD

Purpose

Places characters into the type-ahead keyboard buffer. dBASE IV accepts the characters as if they had been typed in.

Command Syntax

KEYBOARD <*expC*> [CLEAR]

From the dot prompt

Issue the **KEYBOARD** command from the dot prompt or from within a program, specifying the characters to be placed into the keyboard buffer.

LABEL FORM

Purpose

Prints labels for the open datafile.

Command Syntax

LABEL FORM <*label-file-name*>**/?** [SAMPLE] [<*scope*>] [FOR <*condition*>] [WHILE <*condition*>] [TO PRINTER/TO FILE <*file-name*>]

From the dot prompt

1. Issue the CREATE LABEL command to define the label format.
2. After the label is saved on disk, issue a LABEL FORM command.
3. Send the label to the printer by including the TO PRINT clause in the LABEL FORM command.

From the Control Center

1. Open the datafile, and then create and save the label form.
2. If the label form is on disk already, position the bounce bar on the option in the Labels column. Select the Print Label option from the open window.

Note

Adjust the distance between labels by selecting the Spaces Between Label Columns option from the Dimensions submenu.

LIST

Purpose

Sends information to the screen, printer, or disk file.

Command Syntax

LIST/DISPLAY [[FIELDS] <*expression-list*>]
[OFF] {<*scope*>] [FOR <*condition*>]
[WHILE<*condition*>] [TO PRINTER/TO FILE
<*file-name*>]

LIST/DISPLAY FILES [LIKE <*skeleton*>] [TO PRINTER/TO FILE <*file-name*>]

LIST/DISPLAY HISTORY [LAST <*expN*>] [TO PRINTER/TO FILE <*file-name*>]

LIST/DISPLAY STATUS/MEMORY [TO PRINTER/ TO FILE <*file-name*>]

LIST/DISPLAY STRUCTURE [IN <*alias*>] [TO PRINTER/TO FILE <*file-name*>]

LIST/DISPLAY USERS

From the dot prompt

1. Open a datafile. Type **LIST** and press **Enter**. All records in the file scroll up the screen.
2. Type **DISPLAY ALL** and press **Enter**.
3. Type **GO TOP** and press **Enter** to return to the first record in the datafile. Then issue the **DISPLAY** command with a field name.
4. Type **LIST NAME** and press **Enter**. Only the NAME field for all records appears.
5. Type **DISPLAY STATUS** and press **Enter**.
6. Press **Enter** until the dot prompt returns on-screen.
7. Type **LIST STRUCTURE** and press **Enter**. The structure of the open datafile appears on-screen.

From the Control Center

1. Position the bounce bar on the datafile and press **Enter**.
2. A window of options opens on-screen. Select the Display Data option. Use the Browse screen to review and/or change the data.

3. Press **Esc** to return to the Control Center screen without saving the changes.

Notes

Use the **LIST/DISPLAY FILES** command like the **DIR** command.

Type **DISPLAY HISTORY** to display the last several commands issued from the dot prompt.

LOAD

Purpose

Reads a binary program from the disk into memory.

Command Syntax

LOAD *<binary-file-name>*

From the dot prompt

Issue the **LOAD** command to read the binary program from the disk.

Note

You must read the program from disk into memory with the **LOAD** command. Run the program by issuing a **CALL** command. Then remove it from memory with the **RELEASE MODULE** command.

LOCATE

Purpose

Looks through the open file for a specific value.

Command Syntax

LOCATE [FOR] *<condition-1>* [*<scope>*] [WHILE *<condition-2>*]

CONTINUE

From the dot prompt

1. Open the datafile with or without its index file.
2. Issue a **LOCATE** command.

   When the dot prompt returns, display the record to verify the result of the search.
3. Find the next record matching the condition by issuing the **CONTINUE** command.

From the Control Center

1. Open the datafile. Press **Enter** to move the bounce bar to the field you want to search.
2. Press **F10** to access the menu at the top of the screen. Then move right to the Go To option.
3. Press ↓ to position the bounce bar on the Forward Search option and press **Enter**.
4. When asked for the search string, type it in the input area and press **Enter**.

Note

Use a memory variable to provide a changeable search value.

LOGOUT

Purpose

Ends the current session and returns to the sign-on screen from a dBASE IV application.

Command Syntax

LOGOUT

From the dot prompt

Insert the LOGOUT command in the network main menu of the application program. When this command is encountered, it ends the application.

Notes

Issue the PROTECT command when beginning the dBASE IV session. This procedure establishes the log-in verification functions and sets the user access level.

If the PROTECT command was not used during the dBASE IV session, the user is returned to the dot prompt rather than the log-in screen.

MODIFY APPLICATION

See *CREATE APPLICATION*.

MODIFY COMMAND/FILE

Purpose

Used to write or change a dBASE IV program.

Command Syntax

MODIFY COMMAND/FILE <*file-name*> [WINDOW <*window-name*>]

From the dot prompt

1. Issue **MODIFY COMMAND** from the dot prompt and press **Enter**.
2. Press **PgDn**, **PgUp**, **Home**, and **End** to move the cursor through the program. If you make changes, save them by pressing **Ctrl-End**. Otherwise, press **Esc**.
3. Run the program by issuing the **DO** command.

From the Control Center

Select <CREATE> from the Applications panel, and then select dBASE Program to create a new program file.

To edit an existing file, select the file from the Applications menu, and then select Modify Application.

MODIFY LABEL

See *CREATE/MODIFY LABEL.*

MODIFY QUERY/VIEW

See *CREATE/MODIFY QUERY/VIEW*.

MODIFY REPORT

See *CREATE/MODIFY REPORT*.

MODIFY SCREEN

See *CREATE/MODIFY SCREEN*.

MODIFY STRUCTURE

See *CREATE or MODIFY STRUCTURE*.

MOVE WINDOW

See *DEFINE WINDOW*.

NOTE

Purpose

Provides information to anyone who reviews the application program and uses program documentation to describe complicated sections of commands.

Command Syntax

NOTE/* *<text>* [*<command>*] **&&** *<text>*

From the dot prompt

The dBASE IV sample program lines open the SALES data and index files. It ignores all comment lines.

Notes

Issue the **NOTE** command and ***** (asterisk) at the beginning of a program command line.

Use the **&&** symbols to provide documentation after a command. dBASE IV performs the command and ignores everything after the && symbols.

ON ERROR, ESCAPE, KEY

Purpose

Traps errors or recognizes certain keys encountered while the program is running.

Command Syntax

ON ERROR/ESCAPE [<*commands*>]

ON KEY [LABEL <*key-label-name*>] [<*commands*>]

From the dot prompt

1. Include the **ON ERROR** command at the beginning of the program. If an error occurs, the command, procedure, or function included in the command line is performed immediately.
2. Use the **ON ESCAPE** command to identify a command, procedure, or function to be performed when the user presses **Esc**. Display a message to tell the user about the Esc option so that the user is aware of the option.

3. Include the **ON KEY** command to specify a key and a procedure or program to be performed when the user presses the key included in the command line. Specify the key, except the Esc key, in this command.

Note

Include these commands in the beginning of the program to set the trap. It is not processed unless the situation occurs while the application is running.

ON PAD

Purpose

Identifies a pop-up menu to be associated with the menu option on a menu bar.

Command Syntax

ON PAD <*pad-name*> **OF** <*menu-name*> [ACTIVATE POPUP <*popup-name*>]

From the dot prompt

1. Combine the **DEFINE MENU**, **DEFINE PAD**, **DEFINE POPUP**, and **DEFINE BAR** commands to define the menus.
2. Include the **ON PAD** command line to identify the pop-up menu associated with the menu option.

From the Control Center

The Applications Generator handles menu operation automatically.

Note

Include the **RELEASE POPUPS** command in the program to remove the menu definition from memory. Otherwise, you may experience an `Insufficient Memory` error while running an application.

ON PAGE

Purpose

Identifies a command or string of commands to perform when a specified line on a printed page is reached.

Command Syntax

ON PAGE [AT LINE <*expN*> <*commands*>]

From the dot prompt

1. Include the **ON PAGE** command line before printing.
2. Issue an **ON PAGE** command without the optional clauses to disengage the page handler.

ON READERROR

Purpose

Traps errors that occur during data entry.

Command Syntax

ON READERROR [<*commands*>]

From the dot prompt

Include the **ON READERROR** command in programs that edit the datafile.

Note

The trap is not processed unless the situation occurs while you are running the application.

ON SELECTION PAD

See *DEFINE MENU/DEFINE PAD*.

ON SELECTION POPUP

See *DEFINE POPUP*.

PACK

See *DELETE*.

PARAMETERS

Purpose

Passes values from programs or procedures to procedures or functions for additional processing, and often returns new values to the originating program or procedure.

Command Syntax

PARAMETERS *<parameter-list>*

From the dot prompt

1. Write a program that includes a procedure or function that requires information from a calling procedure. The Headers procedure in the following command lines, for example, uses a function called Centered. The procedure sends the width of the page and the value to be centered on that page as parameters. The function includes the PARAMETERS command to accept the information from the calling procedure:

```
procedure headers

lncnt = 5

@lncnt, 01 say date( )

mtemp = "ABC MAIL-OUT COMPANY"

@lncnt, 70 say "Page"

pagecnt = pagecnt + 1

@ lncnt, 75 say pagecnt pict "999"

lncnt = lncnt + 1

mtemp = "Subscription Report for
   "+dtoc(mfrom)+ " thru "+dtoc

(mto)

@ lncnt, centered (80, mtemp)
   say mtemp

lncnt = lncnt + 3

@ lncnt, 10 say "name"

@ lncnt, 35 say "Phone #"

lncnt = lncnt + 3

return
```

```
function centered( )

parameters mcols, mvalue

mnum = ((mcols-len (mvalue)) /2)

return (mnum)
```

2. The procedure passes the report width of 80 and the value to be positioned to the CENTERED() function. It calculates and returns the column position needed to center the value across the page.

Note

Use the PARAMETER command line as the first line of a procedure or function that expects information from the calling program.

PLAY MACRO

Purpose

Performs a macro that is held in memory.

Command Syntax

PLAY MACRO *<macro-name>*

From the dot prompt

Include the **RESTORE** and **PLAY** commands in programs that use macros. The RESTORE command reads the specified file of macros from the disk. To play the macro, issue the **PLAY** command.

From the Control Center

1. Select the Load Library option from the Tools/ Macros submenus.
2. Play the macro by pressing **Alt-F10** and press the key that you assigned to the macro held in memory.

Caution

If you restore a macro file that includes key assignments that already exist in memory, the new macro definition replaces the existing macro.

PRINTJOB/ENDPRINTJOB

Purpose

Controls printing activity. Use it to send print codes (type fonts), eject a page, initialize, and activate dBASE IV system memory variables used to print a report.

Command Syntax

PRINTJOB

<commands>

ENDPRINTJOB

From the dot prompt

Include the PRINTJOB command set in a report program. The PRINTJOB command line identifies the starting point for the report. The ENDPRINTJOB command line identifies the ending point. All command lines between the PRINTJOB and

ENDPRINTJOB commands are processed as part of the printjob set.

From the Control Center

This capability is provided automatically when printing a report from the Report column of the Control Center.

Notes

Report forms include the printjob capabilities automatically. Set the number of copies(_pcopies) before issuing the REPORT FORM command. Page ejection responds to the setting of _pscodes, _pecodes, and _peject.

Do not include a PRINTJOB command set within another printjob. dBASE IV does not allow nesting activity.

PRIVATE

Purpose

Identifies private memory variables and arrays that are to be available only to the program that created them or to the programs run by that program.

Uses PUBLIC to identify variables and arrays that are created and used throughout the application until RELEASE or QUIT is encountered.

Command Syntax

PRIVATE ALL [LIKE/EXCEPT <*skeleton*>]

PRIVATE <*memvar-list*>

PUBLIC <*memory-variable-list*>/[ARRAY <*array-definition-list*>]

From the dot prompt

1. Use the following command lines to create private memory variables called mname and mnum:

```
*    TEST1.PRG - A sample program
     to test private memory
     variables.

*

private mname,mnum

mname = "Jerry"

mnum = 9
```

2. Use the **PUBLIC** command if the variables are needed throughout the application:

```
*    TEST1.PRG - A sample program
     to test private memory
     variables.

*

public mname,mnum

mname = "Jerry"

mnum = 9
```

Notes

When the program that created the private memory variables and arrays has completed its run, its private memory variables are released immediately.

Public variables and arrays are available at any time, to any program, while you are running the application. Private variables and arrays are available only to the current program.

When a variable is declared as public, its value can be changed by any program.

PROCEDURE

Purpose

Writes a program in sections to perform specialized tasks.

Command Syntax

PROCEDURE *<procedure-name>*

From the dot prompt

1. Use the **PROCEDURE** command to identify small programs called by a main program. Include the **PARAMETERS** command line in a program or procedure to accept information from the calling program.
2. Issue the **DO** command to perform a procedure.

Note

A procedure file contains several programs. A program that uses procedure files runs faster than one that uses separate programs.

PROTECT

Purpose

Restricts access to dBASE IV, datafiles, or fields in any of the following ways:

Log-in	Provides access to dBASE IV to authorized personnel only.

File and/or Field	Authorizes access to certain files, and/or fields of dBASE IV files.
Data Encryption	Changes all data within the protected file so that unauthorized users cannot read it.

Command Syntax

PROTECT

From the dot prompt

1. Issue the **PROTECT** command line to access its submenus.
2. Type and verify the database password of the administrator.
3. Use the Users submenu to assign which users can use dBASE IV.
4. Change to the Files submenu.
5. Open the Reports submenu to review user security levels.
6. When you complete all protection activity, use the Exit submenu to Save, Abandon, or Exit the protection menus and return to the dot prompt.

From the Control Center

1. Press **F10** to access the menu at the top of the screen.
2. Choose Tools/Protect Data.
3. Follow steps 2-6 in the dot prompt procedure to make protection changes.

PUBLIC

See *PRIVATE*.

QUIT

Purpose

Ends the current dBASE IV session.

Command Syntax

QUIT [WITH *<expN>*]

From the dot prompt

Type QUIT and press Enter.

From the Control Center

1. Press F10 to access the menu line at the top of the screen.
2. Select the Quit to DOS option from the Exit submenu.

Notes

The optional WITH expression may be used to return an integer value to the calling program or operating system.

Although you can use QUIT to close all open data files, it is better to issue the USE or CLOSE DATABASES command prior to issuing QUIT.

READ

See *@...SAY, GET.*

RECALL

Purpose

Removes the deletion flag for records in a database.

Command Syntax

RECALL [<*scope*>] [FOR <*condition*>] [WHILE <*condition*>]

From the dot prompt

1. Open a datafile. Use the **GO** command to move to the record you want to recall.
2. Display the record to ensure that the current record is the correct one. The * (asterisk) between the record number and the first field value identifies this record for removal.
3. Type **RECALL** and press **Enter**. You are told that one record is recalled (unmarked). Display the record to verify the result.

From the Control Center

1. Open a datafile and press **F2** to use the Browse screen.
2. Move the bounce bar to the deleted record in the datafile.
3. Press **F10** to access the menu line at the top of the screen. Select Clear Deletion Mark to unmark the current record.

4. Select the Exit option from the Exit submenu to return to the Control Center.

Note

Use RECALL ALL to unmark all records flagged for deletion.

REINDEX

See *INDEX*.

RELEASE

Purpose

Releases the memory variables, modules, menus, pop-up menus, and windows held in memory.

Command Syntax

RELEASE <*memvar-list*>

RELEASE ALL [LIKE/EXCEPT<*skeleton*>]

RELEASE MODULES [<*module-name-list*>]

/MENUS [<*menu-name-list*>]

/POPUPS [<*popup-name-list*>]

/SCREENS [<*screen-name-list*>]

/WINDOWS [<*window-name-list*>]

From the dot prompt

1. Use **RELEASE ALL** to free up all the memory used by memory variables.

2. Use **RELEASE MENUS** to free up the memory used by pop-up menus.
3. Use **RELEASE POPUPS** to free up the memory used by pop-up menus.
4. Use **RELEASE SCREENS** to free up the memory used by screen displays.
5. Use **RELEASE WINDOWS** to free up all memory used by windows.
6. Use **RELEASE MODULES** to remove a LOADed program from memory.

Notes

When releasing MENUS, POPUPS, SCREENS, WINDOWS, or MODULES, you may list the individual name(s) to release.

Include the **RELEASE** command in the program to remove the menu definition from memory. Otherwise, you may experience an `Insufficient Memory` error while running an application.

RENAME

Purpose

Changes the name of files on your disk without ending the dBASE IV session.

Command Syntax

RENAME *<old-file-name>* **TO** *<new-file-name>*

From the dot prompt

Issue the **RENAME** command.

From the Control Center

1. Press **F10** to access the menu line at the top of the screen.
2. Select the Tools/DOS Utilities options. A window that contains file names, lengths, date, time, attributes, and space used appears on-screen.
3. Press **F10** so that a new menu line and a window of submenu options are included on-screen.
4. Position the bounce bar on the file you want to rename.
5. Open the Operations submenu and select the Rename option. When asked for the new name, type it in the input area.

REPLACE

Purpose

Changes the information in a field for at least one record in the open datafile.

Command Syntax

REPLACE *<field-name>* **WITH** *<exp-1>* [ADDITIVE]
[,*<field-name-2>* WITH *<exp-2>* [ADDITIVE]
[*<scope>*] [REINDEX] [FOR *<condition>*]
[WHILE *<condition>*]

From the dot prompt

1. Open the datafile (with or without specifying an index file) in the USE command line.

2. In this example, change the customer number (C) of the current record so that it contains zeros in the first two of five positions:

   REPLACE CUST_NO WITH "00" + RIGHT(CUST_NO,3)

3. To change all values in the MTD_SALES (month-to-date sales figures) field to zero, use the following command:

   REPLACE ALL MTD_SALES WITH 0

4. Include a conditional clause to limit the number of replacements.

5. Change the values of several fields in a record by stringing the fields on one line.

From the Control Center

1. Open the datafile.

2. Select the Create option from the Queries column.

3. Remove the view by pressing **F5**.

4. Press **F10** and select the Specify Update option from the Update submenu. Another submenu window opens on-screen.

5. Select the Replace Values option. When the submenus disappear, "Replace" appears in the first column of the query line.

6. Press **Tab** to move to the column you want to replace with other values, and then type the condition.

7. Reopen the Update submenu and select Perform the Update.

Notes

When two datafiles with the same field name are open during a replace operation, specify the work area by a letter (A, B, C,...) or an alias name.

When values are replaced in the datafile, the only way to return the data to its original value is by using BEGIN/END TRANSACTION and ROLLBACK.

REPLACE FROM ARRAY

Purpose

Replaces fields in database records with data stored in an array.

Command Syntax

REPLACE FROM ARRAY *<array name>* [*<scope>*] [REINDEX] [FIELDS *<field-list>] [FOR <condition>] [WHILE <condition>]*

From the dot prompt

1. Open the datafile with the USE command.
2. Issue the REPLACE FROM ARRAY command, optionally specifying the fields to be replaced (using the FIELDS option or using the SET FIELDS command) and the records to be affected (using the scope, FOR and WHILE clauses). The default scope is the current record only.

REPORT FORM

Purpose

Reports on information contained in your dBASE IV databases. Reports can be columnar, special forms, or mailmerge documents.

Command Syntax

REPORT FORM *<report-form-file-name>* /? [PLAIN] [HEADING]*<expC>*] [NOEJECT] [SUMMARY] [*<scope>*] [FOR *<condition>*] [WHILE *<condition>*] [TO PRINTER/TO FILE *<file-name>*]

From the dot prompt

1. Open the datafiles required by the report format.
2. Issue the REPORT FORM command and press Enter. The report appears on-screen.
3. Include the TO PRINT clause to send the report to the printer and print each record from the database on paper.

From the Control Center

1. Open the datafiles needed by the report form.
2. Position the bounce bar on the Report Form option of the Reports column and press Enter. Select the Print Report option.
3. Another window of print options opens on-screen. Select the Begin Printing option to send the information to the printer.

Notes

Use the FOR and WHILE clauses to limit the records printed on the report.

Use the NOEJECT option to combine several reports on the same page.

RESET

Purpose

Resets integrity tag in a file.

Command Syntax

RESET [IN <*alias*>]

From the dot prompt

1. Write a datafile processing program that includes the BEGIN TRANSACTION, END TRANSACTION command set. Include the BEGIN TRANSACTION command line to identify the starting point for the transaction processing. The END TRANSACTION command marks the end.
2. Use the ROLLBACK command to restore the database file to its pretransaction state.
3. Use the RESET command line to tag the files involved in transaction processing.

Notes

Identify the necessary processing to be changed before using the RESET command.

The ROLLBACK command is effective for the APPEND, BROWSE, CHANGE, DELETE, EDIT, RECALL REPLACE, and UPDATE commands. You also can create new files by using the **COPY**, **CREATE**, **IMPORT FROM**, **INDEX**, **JOIN**, **SET CATALOG**, **SORT**, and **TOTAL** commands. Overwriting files or closing open files is not allowed if you intend to use the rollback capability.

Do not include the CLEAR ALL, CLOSE, DELETE FILE, ERASE, INSERT, MODIFY STRUCTURE, PACK, RENAME, or ZAP commands in transaction processing.

RESTORE

Purpose

Restores memory variables, macros, and windows from disk files, or screen images from memory.

Command Syntax

RESTORE FROM *<file-name>* [ADDITIVE]

RESTORE MACROS FROM *<macro-file>*

RESTORE SCREEN FROM *<screen-name>*

RESTORE WINDOW *<window-name-list>*/ALL
FROM *<file-name>*

From the dot prompt

1. Save memory variables to a file with the command **SAVE TO** *<file-name>*. Restore them with the **RESTORE FROM** *<file-name>* command.
2. Issue one of the **RESTORE** commands to read information from disk into memory.

3. Issue the RESTORE SCREEN FROM command to replace the current screen image with one stored in memory.

From the Control Center

1. Use the Load Library option from the Tools/ Macros submenus to read a macro file from disk.
2. Press Alt-F10 to play the macro, and then type the key that you assigned to the recorded macro.

Note

If you restore a macro file that includes key assignments that already exist in memory, the new macro definition replaces the existing macro.

RESUME

Purpose

Causes suspended programs to resume execution at the point they were suspended.

Command Syntax

RESUME

From the dot prompt

1. Include the SUSPEND command in a program to stop the program temporarily. The dot prompt is available for you to display or change memory variables, datafile records, or any combination of information.

2. When you are ready to continue the program as though it had not been stopped, use the **RESUME** command from the dot prompt. The program continues running each command.

Note

All memory variables, files, and so on are available after processing the SUSPEND command. Use the **?** and **DISPLAY** commands to display the values of variables and fields.

RETRY

Purpose

Retries executing a program that dBASE IV determines has an error.

Command Syntax

RETRY

From the dot prompt

Include the **ON ERROR DO** *<file-name>* **WITH ERROR()** command to handle errors encountered after the command. The RETRY command tells dBASE IV to try the command again.

```
ON ERROR DO FIXIT WITH ERROR ()

USE AFILE


*FIXIT.PRG

PARAMETERS Error
```

```
IF Error = 3
  CLOSE DATABASE
ENDIF
RETRY
```

Note

The RETRY command usually is included in an error recovery program.

RETURN

Purpose

Stops a program and returns to the calling program or dot prompt.

Command Syntax

RETURN [<*expression*>/**TO MASTER**/**TO** <*procedure*>]

From the dot prompt

1. Review the following command syntax for the RETURN command:

```
Mfrom = Date()
Mto = Date()
USE subscrpt ORDER subscrpt
@ 08, 15 TO 14, 60 DOUBLE COLOR R/W
@ 09, 16 FILL TO 13, 59 COLOR W/N
@ 10, 20 SAY "Enter the beginning date"
```

```
GET Mfrom PICTURE "99/99/99"
@ 12, 20 SAY "Enter the ending date
" GET Mto PICTURE "99/99/99"
READ
IF Mto- Mfrom > 366
    @ 21, 01 SAY "The date range
      is longer than one year -
      aborting the request..."
      WAIT
   RETURN
ENDIF
```

2. Use the **RETURN** command to cause the current program to send control back to the program or dot prompt that ran the program containing this command.

Notes

If the RETURN command is encountered without the optional clauses, the processing of the current program ends. Processing resumes with the program that called that program, after the line that made the call.

When the [TO MASTER] clause is included, processing continues with the highest level calling program.

Enclose each of these commands within an **IF**, **ENDIF**, or **DO CASE**, **ENDCASE** command set. Otherwise the RETURN is encountered immediately.

ROLLBACK

See *BEGIN/END TRANSACTION*.

RUN/!

Purpose

Performs operations available from the DOS prompt.

Command Syntax

RUN *<DOS-commands>*

! *<DOS-commands>*

From the dot prompt

Issue the **RUN** command to perform a program without leaving the dBASE IV session.

From the Control Center

1. Press **F10** to access the menu line at the top of the screen. Select the Tools/DOS Utilities options. A window that contains file names, lengths, date, time, and space attributes appears on-screen.
2. Open the DOS submenu. Select the Perform DOS Command option to issue and run a DOS command from the Control Center.
3. Select the Go to DOS option to suspend the dBASE prompt. Issue and run the desired DOS commands.
4. Type **EXIT** and press **Enter** to return to the Control Center screen.

Note

The ! command is a shorthand version of the RUN command. Use either of these commands to run a

DOS command or another program from the dBASE IV dot prompt.

SAVE

Purpose

Saves memory variables, macros, and windows to disk, and saves screen images to memory.

Command Syntax

SAVE TO *<file-name>* [ALL LIKE/EXCEPT *<skeleton>*]

SAVE MACROS TO *<macro-file>*

SAVE WINDOW *<window-name-list>* /ALL TO *<file-name>*

From the dot prompt

1. Create the memory variables, macros, and/or windows.
2. Use a SAVE command to save all the information on disk, or use the SAVE SCREEN command to save the screen image in memory.

From the Control Center

1. Create the macros you want to save to disk.
2. Select the Save Library option from the Tools/Macros submenus to write the current macros to the disk.

Notes

If you restore a macro file that includes key assignments that already exist in memory, the new macro definition replaces the existing macro.

If you restore a memory variable, or window file, the variables and windows in memory when the RESTORE command is encountered are overlaid unless you specify the ADDITIVE option.

SCAN, ENDSCAN

Purpose

Performs a set of command lines several times within a program.

Command Syntax

SCAN [<*scope*>] [FOR <*condition*>]
    [WHILE<*condition*>]
    [<*commands*>...]
    [LOOP]
    [EXIT]

ENDSCAN

From the dot prompt

Include the SCAN, ENDSCAN command set rather than the DO WHILE, ENDDO command set in a program. Because the record pointer moves in this command set automatically, do not include the SKIP command.

From the Control Center

Looping is done automatically when you use selections from the Queries, Forms, Reports, and Labels columns.

Notes

Use the **SCAN**, **ENDSCAN** command set to perform a loop. Each command set specifies at least one condition that must be met for the loop to continue processing.

The SCAN, ENDSCAN command set is similar to the DO WHILE, ENDDO command set; however, SCAN, ENDSCAN is always used to process a datafile. Therefore, this command set handles the movement of the record pointer and knows when it has reached the end of the file.

SEEK

Purpose

dBASE IV looks through the data in the open file for specific information.

Command Syntax

SEEK *<expression>*

From the dot prompt

1. Open the datafile with its index file.
2. Issue a **SEEK** command with the expression to seek.

3. When the dot prompt returns, use the **DISPLAY** command to display the records.

4. Create a memory variable (MKEY), and then issue the **SEEK MKEY** command line to begin the search.

From the Control Center

1. Open the datafile and press **F2** to display the data. Press **Enter** to move the bounce bar to the field you want to search.

2. Press **F10** to access the menu at the top of the screen. Open the Go To submenu and select Index Key Search and press **Enter**.

3. When you are asked for the search string, type it in the input area and press **Enter**.

Notes

The search value for the SEEK command may be any valid data type. A memory variable is not required but gives programs more flexibility.

Upper- and lowercase letters must be considered when providing search criteria. If the Go To menu's Match Capitalization option equals Yes, the case must match.

If you prefer to search the datafile for a value or its nearest value, use the **SET NEAR ON** environment command. If the specified value does not exist, dBASE IV returns the nearest match rather than an end-of-file condition.

When using a search command in a program, use the **EOF()** or **FOUND()** functions in an IF command to determine whether the desired record was found during the search. Otherwise, you may be processing the wrong record.

SELECT

Purpose

Enables you to choose a work area in which to open or use a database file.

Command Syntax

SELECT *<work-area-name/alias>*

From the dot prompt

The proper syntax for the USE, CLOSE, and SELECT commands is as follows:

1. Open the datafile with the **USE** command.
2. Type **BROWSE** and press **Enter**. The Browse screen appears. Press **Esc** to return to the dot prompt.
3. Type **SELECT 2**, and then press **Enter** to access another work area. Then open another datafile.
4. Type **BROWSE** and press **Enter**. The data that appears on-screen is from the second datafile. Press **Esc** to return to the dot prompt.
5. Type **CLOSE DATABASES** and press **Enter** to close all open datafiles.

From the Control Center

The work areas for multiple datafiles are handled automatically when you create or open a database.

SET

Purpose

Changes the dBASE IV defaults for colors that appear on-screen, sets the number of decimal places for numbers, and performs other functions.

Command Syntax

SET

From the dot prompt

1. Type **SET** and press **Enter**. The Environment menu of options appears on-screen. Use the arrow keys to position the cursor on the desired option and press **Enter** to select it.
2. Continue to press **Enter** to change the setting in the menu.
3. When all environment options are set, press **Esc** to return to the dot prompt. You can use any of the SET commands from the dot prompt.

From the Control Center

1. Press **F10** to access the menu line at the top of the Control Center.
2. Select the Tools/Setting/Options submenu lines from each window. The environment settings appear in a window.
3. Use the arrow keys to position the bounce bar on the option you want and press **Enter** to select it for changes.

4. To change color selections also, use the Tools/Settings/Display submenu.
5. When all options are set, open the Exit submenu or press **Esc** to exit the Control Center.

Notes

Use the Display submenu to change the screen specifications.

Use the Keys submenu to assign commands to the function keys.

Default settings appear in uppercase letters in the following list of SET commands:

SET ALTERNATE on/**OFF**

SET ALTERNATE TO [<*file-name*> [ADDITIVE]]

SET AUTOSAVE on/**OFF**

SET BELL ON/off

SET BELL TO [<*freq*>,<*duration*>]

SET BLOCKSIZE TO <*expN*>

SET BORDER TO [SINGLE/DOUBLE/PANEL/NONE/<*definition*>]

SET CARRY on/**OFF**

SET CARRY TO [<*field-name-list*> [ADDITIVE]]

SET CATALOG on/**OFF**

SET CATALOG TO [<*file-name*>]

SET CENTURY on/**OFF**

SET CLOCK on/**OFF**

SET CLOCK TO [<*row*>,<*column*>]

SET COLOR ON/OFF

SET COLOR TO [[<*standard*>] [, [<*enhanced*>] [, [<*perimeter*>] [, [<*background*>]]]]]

SET COLOR OF NORMAL/MESSAGES/TITLES/ BOXES/HIGHLIGHT/INFORMATION FIELDS TO [<*attribute*>]

SET CONFIRM on/**OFF**

SET CONSOLE ON/off

SET CURRENCY TO [<*expC*>]

SET CURRENCY LEFT/right

SET CURSOR ON/off

SET DATE AMERICAN/ansi/british/french/german/ italian/japan/usa/mdy/dmy/ymd

SET DBTRAP ON/off

SET DEBUG on/**OFF**

SET DECIMALS TO <*expN*>

SET DEFAULT TO <*drive*> [:]

SET DELETED on/**OFF**

SET DELIMITERS on/**OFF**

SET DELIMITERS TO <*expC*>/**DEFAULT**

SET DESIGN ON/off

SET DEVELOPMENT ON/off

SET DEVICE TO SCREEN/printer/file <*file-name*>

SET DIRECTORY TO [[<*drive*>] [<*path*>]]

SET DISPLAY TO MONO/COLOR/EGA25/ EGA43/ MONO43

SET DOHISTORY on/**OFF**

SET ECHO on/**OFF**

SET ENCRYPTION ON/off

SET ESCAPE ON/off

SET EXACT on/**OFF**

SET EXCLUSIVE on/**OFF**

SET FIELDS on/**OFF**

SET FIELDS TO [<*field-1*> [/R]/ <*calculated- field-1*>...] [, <*field-2*> [/R]/ <*calculated-field-2*>...]

SET FIELDS TO ALL [LIKE/except <*skeleton*>]

SET FILTER TO [FILE <*file-name*>/?] [<*condition*>]

SET FIXED on/**OFF**

SET FORMAT TO [<*format-file-name*>/?]

SET FULLPATH on/**OFF**

SET FUNCTION <*expN*>/<*expC*>/<*key label*> **TO** <*expC*>

SET HEADINGS ON/off

SET HELP ON/off

SET HISTORY ON/off

SET HISTORY TO <*expN*>

SET HOURS TO [12/24]

SET INDEX TO [<*index-file-name-list*>/?] [ORDER <*index-file-name*>/<*multiple-index-tag*> [OF <*multiple-index-file-name*>]]]

SET INSTRUCT ON/off

SET INTENSITY ON/off **SET KEY TO** [<*exp-match*> /RANGE <*exp-low*>,<*exp-high*>/<*exp-low*> [,]/, <*exp-high*>] [IN <*alias*>]

SET KEY TO [<*exp-match*> /RANGE <*exp-low*>,<*exp-high*>/<*exp-low*>[,]/,<*exp-high*>] [IN <alias>]

SET LIBRARY TO <*file-name*>

SET LOCK ON/off

SET MARGIN TO <*expN*>

SET MARK TO [<*expC*>]

SET MEMOWIDTH TO <*expN*>

SET MENU ON/off

SET MESSAGE TO [*<expC>* [AT *<expN>*[,*<expN>*]]]

SET NEAR on/**OFF**

SET ODOMETER TO *<expN>*

SET ORDER TO *<expN>*/*<index-file>*/[TAG] *<tag-name>* [OF *<multiple-index-file>*] [NOSAVE]

SET PATH TO [*<path-list>*]

SET PAUSE on/**OFF**

SET POINT TO [*<expC>*]

SET PRECISION TO [*<expN>*]

SET PRINTER on/**OFF**

SET PRINTER TO *<DOS-device>*

SET PRINTER TO *<computer-name>*/*<printer-name>* = *<destination>*/**SPOOLER**/\\ **CAPTURE**

SET PRINTER TO FILE *<file-name>*

SET PROCEDURE TO [*<procedure-file-name>*]

SET REFRESH TO *<expN>*

SET RELATION TO [*<expression>* INTO *<alias>* [, *<expression>* INTO *<alias>* ...]]

SET REPROCESS TO *<expN>*

SET SAFETY ON/off **SET SCOREBOARD ON**/off **SET SEPARATOR TO** [*<expC>*]

SET SKIP TO [*<alias>* [, *<alias-2>*...]]

SET SPACE ON/off

SET SQL on/**OFF**

SET STATUS on/**OFF**

SET STEP on/**OFF**

SET TALK ON/off

SET TITLE ON/off

SET TRAP on/OFF

SET TYPEAHEAD TO <*expN*>

SET UNIQUE on/OFF

SET VIEW TO <*query-file-name*>/<*view-file-name*>/?

SET WINDOW OF MEMO TO <*window-name*>

SHOW MENU

See *DEFINE MENU*.

SHOW POPUP

See *DEFINE POPUP*.

SKIP

Purpose

Moves the current record pointer forward or backward in a database.

Command Syntax

SKIP [<*expN*>] [IN <*alias*>]

From the dot prompt

1. Open a datafile with the USE command.
2. Type DISPLAY and press Enter. The first record in the datafile appears on-screen.

3. Type **SKIP** and press **Enter** to move down to the next record in the datafile. Display the record.
4. Type **SKIP -2** and press **Enter** to move up two records in the file. Display the record to verify the pointer movement.

From the Control Center

1. Position the cursor on a file name in the Data column. Press **F2** to display the data in a Browse screen.
2. Press **F10** to access the menu at the top of the screen. Select the Skip option from the Go To submenu. When asked for the number of records to skip, type **2** and press **Enter**.

Note

Use the **INDEX** or **SORT** command to put the data in other sequences.

SORT

Purpose

Orders the records to make it easy to find information.

Command Syntax

SORT TO <*file-name*> **ON** <*field-1*> [/A] [/C] [/D] [, <*field-2*> [/A] [/C] [/D]...] [ASCENDING/ DESCENDING] [<*scope*>] [FOR <*condition*>] [WHILE <*condition*>]

From the dot prompt

1. Open the datafile. List the records and notice the sequence.
2. Issue the **SORT TO** command to create a datafile of sequenced records.
3. Open and list the data in the sorted file.

From the Control Center

1. Open the datafile. Press **Shift-F2** to display the data structure.
2. Select the Sort Database on Field List option from the Organize submenu.
3. A window opens for you to type the fields to be used for the sort. Type each name and specify it for ascending or descending order.
4. Press **Enter** to begin the sort. Another window opens. Type the file name and press **Enter**.

Note

Do not sort on logical or memo fields.

STORE

Purpose

Creates a new memory variable or saves a value to an existing memory variable or array element.

Reminders

The number of memory variables allowed is established through the MVBLKSIZE and MVMAXBLKS settings. The default settings follow:

```
MVBLKSIZE = 50

MVMAXBLKS = 10
```

The default settings allow a maximum of 500 memory variables. An array uses one memory variable slot. Use the **DECLARE** command to create an array and the **=** or **STORE** command to provide values.

Command Syntax

STORE *<expression>* **TO** *<memvar-list>/<array-element-list>*

<memvar>/<array-element> **=** *<expression>*

From the dot prompt

1. Copy the contents of a field to a memory variable with the **STORE** or **=** command.
2. Create other variables.
3. Display the current memory variables with the **DISPLAY MEMORY** command.

Notes

The data type of memory variable or array is established by the value stored in that memory variable or array.

dBASE IV provides several system memory variables. Set and use any of the following variables:

Variable	Description
_ALIGNMENT	Returns the position of output "LEFT"/"center"/"right".
_BOX	Specifies whether boxes print.

Variable	Description
_INDENT	Returns paragraph indention for the first line of each paragraph.
_LMARGIN	Defines the left margin for the screen and printer.
_PADVANCE	Returns printer form or line feeds.
_PAGENO	Returns the number to be printed on the next page.
_PBPAGE	Returns the first page of the next print job.
_PCOLNO	Returns the column number of the print head.
_PCOPIES	Returns the number of copies to be printed.
_PDRIVER	Provides the desired printer driver.
_PECODE	Provides the ending print control codes.
_PEJECT	Returns when a page eject must occur ("BEFORE"/"after"/"both"/ "none").
_PEPAGE	Returns the page number to end print job.
_PFORM	Activates or identifies a print form file with all print settings.
_PLENGTH	Identifies the printed page length.
_PLINENO	Provides the current line number for the output device.
_PLOFFSET	Returns page left offset for printed output.
_PPITCH	Provides printer pitch "pica"/"elite"/ "condensed"/"DEFAULT".
_PQUALITY	Provides print mode letter quality (.T.) or draft quality (.F.).

Variable	Description
_PSCODE	Returns the starting print control codes.
_PSPACING	Sets the line spacing for printed output (1/2/3).
_PWAIT	Specifies whether a pause between pages is desired.
_RMARGIN	Defines the right margin for the screen and printer.
_TABS	Sets the number of tabs for the word wrap editor, screen, and printer.
_WRAP	Specifies whether word wrapping between margins is desired.

SUM

See *CALCULATE*.

SUSPEND

Purpose

Suspends execution of a dBASE IV program. This command is valuable when debugging programs.

Command Syntax

SUSPEND

From the dot prompt

1. Include the **SUSPEND** command in a program to stop the program temporarily. The dot

prompt is available for you to display or change memory variables, datafile records, or any combination of information.

2. When you are ready to continue the program as though it had not been stopped, use the RESUME command in the program or from the dot prompt. The program continues running each command.

TEXT, ENDTEXT

Purpose

Prints, or displays, a large block of information for the user without the user specifying the exact screen coordinates.

Command Syntax

TEXT

<text-characters>

ENDTEXT

From the dot prompt

1. Include a block of information between the TEXT and ENDTEXT commands.
2. Remove the SET PRINT command to stop the printing activity.

From the Control Center

Draw a window on-screen and type the textual information in it.

Notes

When you use the TEXT command, use the ENDTEXT command to mark the end of the textual information. Otherwise, dBASE IV treats all command lines following the TEXT command as information for the user.

If the information within the TEXT and ENDTEXT commands used on-screen is longer than 24 lines, the information scrolls past the user. To provide a large block of text the user can read, display a screenful of text, issue a **WAIT** command, and then provide the next TEXT, ENDTEXT information.

TOTAL

Purpose

Sums the values of numeric fields of the active database and creates a second database file to hold the results. The numeric fields in the new database have the totals for all records with the same key.

Command Syntax

TOTAL ON <*key-field*> **TO** <*file-name*> [FIELDS <*field-list*>] [<*scope*>] [FOR <*condition*>] [WHILE <*condition*>]

From the dot prompt

1. Open the database (it must contain at least one numeric field).

2. Create an index for the database.

3. Use the **TOTAL** command that specifies the key field used to create the index:

```
USE Invoice
INDEX ON Custno TAG Invoice
TOTAL ON Custno TO Ninvoice
SELECT 2
USE Ninvoice
BROWSE
```

4. List the new datafile. Notice that one record is available for each customer with a sum of all invoice amounts.

Notes

INDEX the original file before using the TOTAL command.

If the summed value is too large for a numeric field, dBASE IV places asterisks in it. Use **MODIFY STRUCTURE** to provide numeric fields that are large enough for the number.

TYPE

Purpose

Displays the contents of a text file. This dBASE IV command differs from the DOS TYPE command by numbering the file and displaying it on-screen, to a printer, or to a new file.

Command Syntax

TYPE *<file-name>* [NUMBER] [TO PRINTER]/[TO FILE *<file-name>*]

From the dot prompt

Send a program or text file to the printer by issuing a command line, and then pressing **Enter**. If the file exists in the root directory of drive C, and the printer is turned on, the document is sent to the printer.

From the Control Center

1. Press **F10** to access the menu line at the top of the screen.
2. Select the Tools/DOS Utilities options. A window that contains file names, lengths, date, time, attributes, and space used appears on-screen.
3. Press **F10** to access the menu line and select the Perform DOS Command option from the DOS submenu.
4. Issue the **DOS TYPE** command with the file name to type.

Notes

Use **TYPE** for standard text files. Do not try to type databases or index files.

A dBASE IV program cannot contain a TYPE command to list itself.

UNLOCK

Purpose

Releases file locks so that other users can access records.

Command Syntax

UNLOCK [ALL/IN <*alias*>]

From the dot prompt

1. Open a database that has been converted to multiuser status.
2. Verify that you have the file locked with the **? FLOCK**() command.
3. Make the changes you want to the database.
4. Free the database with the **UNLOCK** command.

UPDATE

Purpose

Uses data from another database to update fields in the current database by matching records on a key field.

Command Syntax

UPDATE ON <*key-field*> **FROM** <*alias*> **REPLACE** <*field-1*> **WITH** <*expression-1*> [, <*field-2*> WITH <*expression-2*>...] [RANDOM] [REINDEX]

From the dot prompt

1. Open both databases with their indexes.
2. Issue the **UPDATE** command.

From the Control Center

1. Create a query to create a new datafile.
2. Select the Perform the Update Operation option from the Update submenu on the query screen.

Notes

If duplicate records in the database are being updated, the first matching record is the only one replaced.

Do not specify a multifield key in the UPDATE command.

Both files used with the UPDATE command must be indexed on the key field unless the RANDOM option is specified.

Purpose

Opens an existing datafile along with the appropriate index and memo files in one or more work areas.

Command Syntax

USE [<*file-name*>/?] [IN <*work-area-number*>]
[[INDEX <*index-file-list*/*multiple-index-file*>]
[ORDER <*index-file-name*/[TAG] <*tag-name*>
[OF <*multiple-index-file-name*>]] [ALIAS <*alias*>]
[EXCLUSIVE] [NOUPDATE] [NOLOG]
[NOSAVE] [AGAIN]

From the dot prompt

1. Issue the **USE** command with a datafile name to open it.
2. Type **DISPLAY STATUS**. Press **Enter** to list environment information, and then type **SELECT 3**.
3. Open another file with its index.
4. Type **DISPLAY STATUS**. Press **Enter** to verify the indexed file.
5. Open the file with its index and assign an alias name.
6. Type **CLOSE DATABASES**.

From the Control Center

1. Position the bounce bar on the datafile name in the Data column. Press **Enter** twice to open the file.
2. When the Control Center returns to the screen, the file name appears above the line in the Data column. This indicates that the file is open, and any changes made to the file need to be written on the disk.

Purpose

Causes processing to stop until any key is pressed by the user.

Command Syntax

WAIT [<*prompt*>] [TO <*memvar*>]

From the dot prompt

You use the **WAIT** command to stop processing and wait for user input.

Notes

If the TO <*memvar*> option is included in the command line, a character memory variable is created automatically.

This command does not provide control over the user input. Use the @...GET command to restrict the input.

ZAP

Purpose

Removes all records in a datafile.

Command Syntax

ZAP

From the dot prompt

1. Open a datafile. Type **ZAP** and press **Enter** to remove all records from the database. If SET SAFETY is ON, type **Y** for Yes to delete all records.
2. Close the open datafile.

Note

ZAP reclaims disk space that is occupied by deleted records.

dBASE IV FUNCTIONS

Use any of the following special dBASE IV functions to perform a task or provide information.

The dBASE IV function syntax follows:

& *<character-string>* [.]
Returns macro substitution.

ABS(*<expN>*)
Returns absolute value.

ACCESS()
Returns the access level of the current user.

ACOS(*<expN>*)
Returns angle size in radians of a cosine.

ALIAS([*<expN>*])
Returns the alias name of a work area.

ASC(*<expC>*)
Specifies a character to ASCII decimal conversion.

ASIN(*<expN>*)
Returns the angle size in radians of a sine.

AT(*<expC>*, *<expC>*/*<memo>*)
Returns a substring search in a character or memo expression.

ATAN(*<expN>*)
Returns the angle size in radians of a tangent.

ATN2(*<expN-1>*,*<expN-2>*)
Returns the angle size in radians of a sine and cosine.

BAR()
Returns the number of the last selected prompt bar from the active pop-up.

BOF([*<alias>*])
Returns the beginning of file.

CALL(*<expC>*,*<expression>*, [*<expression-list>*])
Executes a LOADed binary program module.

CATALOG()
Returns the active catalog file name.

CDOW(*<expD>*)
Returns the name of the day of the week.

CEILING(*<expN>*)
Returns the smallest integer > or = to specified value.

CERROR()
Returns the number of the last compiler error message.

CHANGE ([*<alias>*])
Determines whether a record has been changed by a network user.

CHR(*<expN>*)
Returns ASCII decimal to character conversion.

CMONTH(*<expD>*)
Returns the name of the month from a date.

COL()
Returns the cursor column position on-screen.

COMPLETED()
Returns whether a transaction is complete.

COS(*<expN>*)
Returns the cosine value of an angle in radians.

CTOD(*<expC>*)
Returns the character to date conversion.

DATE()
Returns the system date (MM/DD/YY).

DAY(*<expD>*)
Returns the day of month number.

DBF([*<alias>*])
Returns the name of the database in USE.

DELETED([*<alias>*])
Determines whether a record is marked for deletion.

DESCENDING([[*<multiple-index-file>*,] *<expN>* [,*<alias>*]])
Determines whether an index tag is created with DESCENDING option.

DGEN(*<expC1>* [, *<expC2>*])
Runs template language program.

DIFFERENCE(*<expC>*,*<expC>*)
Returns the difference between two SOUNDEX() codes.

DISKSPACE()
Specifies the number of free bytes on the default drive.

DMY(*<expD>*)
Converts the date to DD Month YY form.

DOW(*<expD>*)
Returns the day of the week number.

DTOC(*<expD>*)
Returns the date to character conversion.

DTOR(*<expN>*)
Returns the degrees to radians conversion.

DTOS(*<expD>*)
Returns the date to character date conversion for indexing.

EOF([*<alias>*])
Returns the end of file.

ERROR()
Returns the error number of the last error.

EXP(*<expN>*)
Returns the number from its natural log.

FDATE(*<expC>*)
Returns the date a file was last modified.

FIELD(*<expN>*[, *<alias>*])
Returns the names of fields by numbers.

FILE(*<expC>*)
Verifies the existence of a file.

FIXED(*<expN>*)
Converts a floating point number to a binary coded decimal.

FKLABEL(*<expN>*)
Returns the name of a function key from its number.

FKMAX()
Returns the maximum number of programmable function keys.

FLDCOUNT([*<alias>*]
Returns the number of fields in a database structure

FLOAT(*<expN>*)
Converts binary coded decimal numbers to floating point.

FLOCK([*<alias>*])
Locks a database file.

FLOOR(*<expN>*)
Returns the largest integer < or = to the specified value.

FOR()
Returns the condition used for an index tag.

FOUND([*<alias>*])
Returns the logical result of a database search.

FSIZE(*<expC>*)
Returns the size of file in bytes.

FTIME(<*expC*>)
Returns the time the file was last modified.

FV(<*payment*>,<*rate*>,<*periods*>)
Returns the future value of investment at fixed interest for a given time.

GETENV(<*expC*>)
Returns the contents of a DOS environment variable.

HOME()
Returns the path from which dBASE was run.

ID()
Returns the name of the current user on the network.

IIF(<*condition*>,<*exp-1*>,<*exp-2*>)
Returns immediate if.

INKEY()
Returns the decimal ASCII value of the last key pressed.

INT(<*expN*>)
Returns a conversion to an integer by truncating decimals.

ISALPHA(<*expC*>)
Specifies whether the first character is a letter.

ISBLANK(<*exp*>)
Specifies whether an expression is blank.

ISCOLOR()
Checks hardware for color capability.

ISLOWER(<*expC*>)
Specifies whether the first character is lowercase.

ISMARKED([<*alias*>])
Specifies whether the first character is uppercase.

KEY([[<*multiple-index-file*>,] <*expN*> [,<*alias*>]])
Returns a key expression for the specified index file.

LASTKEY()
Returns the decimal ASCII value of the key pressed to exit full-screen command.

LEFT(*<expC>*/*<memo>*,*<expN>*)
Returns the number of characters counting from left of string.

LEN(*<expC>*/*<memo>*)
Returns the number of characters in a specified string or a memo field.

LIKE(*<pattern>*,*<expC>*)
Compares strings using wild-card characters.

LINENO()
Returns the line number to be executed next in current program.

LKSYS(*n*)
Returns the time, date, and log-in name for a locked file.

LOCK([*<expC-list>*] [,*<alias>*])
Locks a datafile record in the network system. See also *RLOCK*.

LOG(*<expN>*)
Returns the natural logarithm of a number.

LOG10(*<expN>*)
Returns the logarithm to base 10.

LOOKUP(*<return-exp>*,*<look-for-exp>*,*<look-in-field>*)
Looks up a record from another database file.

LOWER(*<expC>*)
Converts uppercase letters to lowercase.

LTRIM(<expC>)
Removes leading blanks from a character string.

LUPDATE([*<alias>*])
Returns the last date of file update.

MAX(*<exp-1>*,*<exp-2>*)
Returns the greater of two values.

MDX(*<expN>* [,*<alias>*])
Returns the name of an open .MDX file.

MDY(*<expD>*)
Converts the date format to month DD, YY.

MEMLINES(*<memo-field-name>*)
Returns the number of word-wrapped lines in memo field at current width.

MEMORY([0])
Returns the amount of RAM in kilobytes (optional zero does not affect the result).

MENU()
Returns the name of the active menu.

MESSAGE()
Returns the error message string of the last error.

MIN(*<exp-1>*,*<exp-2>*)
Returns the lesser of two values.

MLINE(*<memo-field-name>*,*<expN>*)
Returns a line of a memo field.

MOD(*<expN-1>*,*<expN-2>*)
Returns the modulus (remainder of numeric expression 1 by expression 2).

MONTH(*<expD>*)
Returns the number of month from a date.

NDX([*<expN>* [,*<alias>*]])
Returns name of an open .NDX file.

NETWORK()
Specifies that dBASE IV is installed and running on a network.

ORDER([*<alias>*])
Returns the name of primary order index file or .MDX tag.

OS()
Specifies the operating system in use.

PAD()
Specifies the selected prompt pad name of the active menu.

PAYMENT(*<principal>*,*<rate>*,*<periods>*)
Specifies the periodic payment on a loan with fixed interest.

PCOL()
Specifies the printer column position.

PCOUNT()
Returns the number of parameters passed to a procedure.

PI()
Specifies the mathematical constant for the ratio of circumference to diameter.

POPUP()
Specifies the name of the active pop-up menu.

PRINTSTATUS()
Returns printer status.

PROGRAM()
Returns the name of program being executed when an error occurs.

PROMPT()
Returns the prompt of the last selected pop-up or menu option.

PROW()
Returns the printer row position.

PV(*<payment>*,*<rate>*,*<periods>*)
Calculates the present value of equal payments invested at fixed interest for a certain number of payment periods.

RAND([*<expN>*])
Returns the random number generator.

READKEY()
Returns the value of key pressed to exit full screen.

RECCOUNT([<*alias*>])
Returns the number of records in the current database file.

RECNO([<*alias*>])
Returns the current record number of a selected datafile.

RECSIZE([<*alias*>])
Returns the size of a record in selected datafile.

REPLICATE(<*expC*>,<*expN*>)
Repeats a character expression a specified number of times.

RIGHT(<*expC*>,<*expN*>)
Returns the number of characters counting from the right of the string.

RLOCK([<*expC-list*>] [,<*alias*>])
Locks at least one datafile record in a network.

ROLLBACK()
Specifies whether the most recent rollback was successful.

ROUND(<*expN-1*>,<*expN-2*>)
Rounds the number in <*expN-1*> to <*expN-2*> decimal places.

ROW()
Returns the row number of the current cursor position.

RTOD(<*expN*>)
Converts radians to degrees.

RTRIM(<*expC*>)
Removes trailing blanks (see *TRIM()*).

RUN([<*exp* <*1*>, [<*expC*>[,<*exp* <*2*>])
Executes an operating system command or program.

SEEK(<*expC*> [,<*alias*>])
Searches indexed datafiles.

SELECT([<*alias*>]
Returns the number of available work areas or the work area number of a specified file.

SET(<*expC*>)
Returns the current settings of the SET commands.

SIGN(<*expN*>)
Returns a mathematical sign of a number or an expression.

SIN(<*expN*>)
Returns a sine from an angle in radians.

SOUNDEX(<*expC*>)
Returns the four-character code used as an index to find possible matches in sound-alike searches.

SPACE(<*expN*>)
Specifies a string made of blank spaces (254 maximum).

SQRT(<*expN*>)
Returns the square root of a specified number.

STR(<*expN*> [,<*length*>] [,<*decimal*>])
Returns a number to character string conversion.

STUFF(<*expC-1*>,<*expN-1*>,<*expN-2*>,<*expC-2*>)
Replaces part of a character string with another character string.

SUBSTR(<*expC*>,<*starting-position*> [,<*number-of-characters*>])
Extracts a specified number or characters from a string or memo field counting from the right.

TAG([<*multiple-index-files*>,] <*expN*> [,<*alias*>])
Returns the tag name in a specified .MDX file.

TAGCOUNT([<*multiple-index-file*> [,<*alias*>]])
Returns the number of active indexes.

TAGNO(<*order-name*> [,<*multiple-index-name*> [,<*alias*>]])
Returns the index tag number.

TAN(<*expN*>)
Returns the tangent from an angle in radians.

TIME()
Returns system time (HH:MM:SS).

TRANSFORM(<*exp*>,<*expC*>)
Returns picture formatting of character, logical, date, and numeric data without using the @ commands.

TRIM(<*expC*>)
Removes trailing blanks. (This is the same as RTRIM().)

TYPE(<*expC*>)
Returns an uppercase C, N, L, M, D, F, or U data type.

UNIQUE([[<*expC*>,] <*expN*> [,<*alias*>]])
Specifies whether an index tag was created with the UNIQUE option.

UPPER(<*expC*>)
Converts lowercase letters to uppercase.

USER()
Returns the log-in name of the network user.

VAL(<*expC*>)
Specifies character to number conversion.

VARREAD()
Returns the name of a field or variable being edited.

VERSION()
Returns the dBASE IV version number in use.

WINDOW()
Returns the name of the active window.

YEAR(<*expD*>)
Returns the year from date expression (YYYY).

LOW-LEVEL FILE I/O FUNCTIONS

Low-level file I/O functions allow the dBASE IV programmer to manipulate operating level binary files. These functions are similar to C language file functions. They work with data stream files at the operating system level and require a knowledge of programming at that level.

FCLOSE(*<expN>*)
Closes a low-level file.

FCREATE(*<expC-1>* [,*<expC-2>*])
Creates a low-level file.

FEOF(*<expN>*)
Returns the end of file status.

FERROR()
Returns the error status of a low-level file operation.

FFLUSH(*<expN>)*
Writes system buffer of a low-level file to disk.

FGETS((*<expN-1>* [,*<expN-2>*] [,*<expC>*])
Reads a character string from a low-level file.

FOPEN((*<expC-1>* [,*<expC-2>*])
Opens a low-level file.

FPUTS(*<expN-1>*,*<expC-1>* [,*<expN-2>*] [,*<expC-2>*])
Writes a character string to a low-level file.

FREAD(*<expN-1>*,*<expN-2>*)
Reads bytes from a low-level file.

FSEEK(*<expN-1>*,*<expN-2>* [,*<expN-3>*])
Moves the file pointer in a low-level file.

FWRITE(*<expN-1>*,*<expC-1>* [,*<expN-2>*])
Writes characters to a low-level file.

SQL COMMAND REFERENCE

The Structured Query Language (SQL) began in the mainframe and minicomputer environment. SQL is an advanced relational database language. The following commands are valid SQL commands:

ALTER TABLE *<table-name>* **ADD** (*<column-name><data-type>*[, *<column-name><data-type>*...]);
Adds new columns to an existing table.

CLOSE *<cursor-name>*;
Closes an SQL cursor.

CREATE DATABASE [*path*] *<datafile>*;
Creates a directory and set of SQL catalog tables for the new SQL datafile.

CREATE [UNIQUE] **INDEX** *<index-name>* **ON** *<table>* (*<column-name>* [ASC/DEXC] [, *<column-name>*...]);
Creates an index based on one or more columns in a table or view.

CREATE SYNONYM *<synonym-name>* **FOR** *<table/view-name>*;
Defines an alternate name for a table or view.

CREATE TABLE *<table-name>* (*<column-name><data-type>*) [, ...];
Creates a new table, defining the columns within that table.

CREATE VIEW *<view-name>*[(*<column-name>*, *<column-name>*...)] **AS** <SELECT-*command*>[WITH CHECK OPTION];
Creates a virtual table based on the columns defined in [*<column-list>*], other tables, or views.

DBCHECK [*<table-name>*];
Verifies that SQL catalog tables contain current SQL tables.

DBDEFINE [*<.dbf-file>*];
Creates SQL catalog table entries for dBASE IV datafiles.

DECLARE *<cursor-name>* **CURSOR FOR** <SELECT *statement*> [FOR UPDATE OF *<column-list>*/ <ORDER BY *clause*>];
Defines a cursor and an associated SELECT statement that specifies a result table for the cursor.

DELETE FROM *<table-name>* [*<alias-name>*] [<WHERE *clause*>];
Deletes specified rows from a table.

DELETE FROM *<table-name>* **WHERE CURRENT OF** *<cursor-name>*;
Deletes the row identified by the cursor.

DROP DATABASE *<datafile-name>*;
Deletes an SQL datafile and removes all datafiles and index files from directory.

DROP INDEX *<index-name>*;
Deletes an existing SQL index.

DROP SYNONYM *<synonym-name>*;
Deletes an SQL synonym name.

DROP TABLE *<table-name>*;
Deletes an SQL table.

DROP VIEW *<view-name>*;
Deletes an SQL view.

FETCH *<cursor-name>* **INTO** *<variable-list>*;
Advances the cursor pointer and copies the values of the selected row into dBASE IV memory variables.

GRANT ALL [PRIVILEGES]/*<privilege-list>* **ON** [TABLE] *<table-list>* **TO PUBLIC**/*<user-list>* [WITH GRANT OPTION];
Grants user access privileges and update privileges of tables and views.

INSERT INTO *<table-name>* [(*<column-list>*)] <SELECT-*command*>;
Inserts rows in a table or updatable view.

INSERT INTO *<table-name>* [(*<column-list>*)] **VALUES** (*<value-list>*);
Inserts rows in a table or updatable view.

LOAD DATA FROM [*path*] *<file-name>* **INTO TABLE** *<table-name>* [[TYPE] **SDF/DIF/WKS/SYLK/FW2/RPD/DBASEII/DELIMITED** [WITH BLANK/WITH *<delimiter>*]];
Imports data into an SQL table from a foreign file.

OPEN *<cursor-name>*;
Opens a cursor and positions the cursor before the first row in the result table.

REVOKE ALL [PRIVILEGES]/*<privileges-list>* **ON** [TABLE] *<table-name>* **FROM PUBLIC**/*<user-list>*;
Removes table access and update privileges.

ROLLBACK [WORK];
Restores a table to its previous contents prior to execution of commands in a BEGIN TRANSACTION, END TRANSACTION command set.

RUNSTATS [*<table-name>*];
Updates statistics in SQL catalog tables of the current datafile.

SELECT <*clause*> [INTO <*clause*>] FROM <*clause*> [WHERE <*clause*>] [GROUP BY <*clause*>] [HAVING <*clause*>] [UNION *subselect*] [ORDER BY <*clause*>/FOR UPDATE OF <*clause*>] [SAVE TO TEMP <*clause*>];
Retrieves data from tables or views.

SHOW DATABASE;
Displays information about SQL database files.

START DATABASE <*database-name*>;
Activates an SQL datafile.

STOP DATABASE;
Deactivates the current active SQL datafile.

UNLOAD DATA TO [*path*] <*file-name*> **FROM TABLE** <*table-name*> [[TYPE] **SDF/DIF/WKS/SYLK/FW2/RPD/DBASEII/DELIMITED** [WITH BLANK/WITH <*delimiter*>]];
Exports data from an SQL table to a foreign file.

UPDATE <*table-name*>/<*view-name*> **SET** <*column-name*> **=** <*expression*>...[WHERE <*search-condition*>];
Changes column values in rows of a table or updateable view.

UPDATE <*table*> **SET** <*column-name*> = <*expression*>,... **WHERE CURRENT OF** <*cursor-name*>;
Changes column values in rows of a table or updatable view.

SQL Functions

The following SQL functions are available through dBASE IV:

AVG ([ALL/DISTINCT] <*column-name*>/<*column-expression*>)
Computes the average value of a numeric column in selected rows.

COUNT ([*/DISTINCT] *<column-name>*)
Counts the number of selected rows in a query.

MAX ([ALL/DISTINCT]] *<column-expression>*/ *<column-name>*)
Returns the maximum value found in specified columns.

MIN ([ALL/DISTINCT] *<column-name>*/*<column-expression>*)
Returns the minimum value found in specified columns.

SUM ([ALL/DISTINCT] *<column-name>*/*<column-expression>*
Sums the values of a numeric column in selected rows.

INDEX

Symbols

! command, 3
&& command, 3
* command, 3
= command, 1
?,??,??? commands, 1-3
@...SAY, GET command, 3-5
@...TO, FILL, CLEAR, SCROLL command, 5-6

A

ACCEPT command, 6-7
ACTIVATE MENU command, 7
ACTIVATE POPUP command, 7
ACTIVATE SCREEN command, 7-8
ACTIVATE WINDOW command, 8
ALTER TABLE ADD() SQL command, 139
APPEND command, 8-9
APPEND FROM command, 9-10
APPEND MEMO command, 11-12
Applications Generator, 27-28
arrays, establishing, 37-38
ASSIST command, 12
AVERAGE command, 12

B

BEGIN/END TRANS command, 13-14
Binary Named List (BNL) files, creating, 46
binary programs, running, 18-19
BLANK command, 14
bounce bar menus, building, 39-40
BROWSE command, 15-17
Browse screen, 33-34
buffers, 68

C

CALCULATE command, 17-18
CALL command, 18-19
CANCEL command, 19-20
CHANGE command, 21
CLEAR command, 21
CLOSE command, 22
CLOSE SQL command, 139
closing
datafiles, 22
programs, 19-20
combining two datafiles, 66-68
command lines, 103-104
COMPILE command, 23-24
CONTINUE command, 24
Control Center screen, 12
CONVERT command, 24-25
COPY command, 25-27
copying records, 25-27
COUNT command, 27
CREATE APPLICATION command, 27-28
CREATE DATABASE SQL command, 139
CREATE FROM command, 28-29
CREATE INDEX ON SQL command, 139
CREATE or MODIFY STRUCTURE command, 35-36
CREATE SYNONYM FOR SQL command, 139

CREATE TABLE SQL command, 139
CREATE VIEW AS SQL command, 140
CREATE/MODIFY LABEL command, 29-30
CREATE/MODIFY QUERY/ VIEW command, 30-31
CREATE/MODIFY REPORT command, 32-33
CREATE/MODIFY SCREEN command, 33-34
creating
- datafile layout, 35-36
- files
  - Binary Named List (BNL) files, 46
  - from non-dBASE software, 63

current session, ending, 73
cursor, positioning, 3-5

D

data
- controlling processing, 61-62
- deleting from screen or memory, 21
- organizing, 64-65

databases
- adding records to, 9-10
- moving record pointer within, 112-113
- numeric fields, summing values, 119-120
- recording changes to, 13-14
- records, removing deletion flags for, 88-89

datafiles
- adding records to, 8-9
- changing
  - data, 15-17
  - from single user to multiuser, 24-25
  - information in, 51-53
  - layout, 35-36
- closing, 22
- combining two, 66-68
- creating
  - from another datafile, 28
  - layout for, 35-36
- designing/printing labels, 29-30
- inserting records, 66
- opening, 123-124
- printing labels, 68-69
- records
  - calculating, 17-18
  - copying, 25-27
  - extracting, 30-31
  - flagging for removal, 44-45
  - printing from open datafiles, 32-33
  - removing, 125
- restricting access to, 85-86
- selecting work areas, 106
- viewing data, 15-17

dBASE IV programs, 48
DBCHECK SQL command, 140
DBDEFINE SQL command, 140
DEACTIVATE MENU command, 36
DEACTIVATE POPUP command, 36
DEACTIVATE WINDOW command, 36
DEBUG command, 36-37
DECLARE command, 37-38
DECLARE CURSOR FOR SQL command, 140
defaults, resetting, 107-112
DEFINE BAR command, 38
DEFINE BOX command, 38-39
DEFINE MENU commands, 39-40
DEFINE PAD command, 39-40
DEFINE POPUP command, 41-42
DEFINE WINDOW command, 42-43
DELETE command, 44-45
DELETE FILE command, 45
DELETE FROM SQL command, 140

DELETE FROM WHERE
CURRENT OF SQL
command, 140
DELETE TAG command, 45-46
deletion flags, removing, 88-89
DEXPORT command, 46
DIR command, 47-48
disks
listing files, 47-48
removing files without
ending session, 54-55
sending information, 69-71
DISPLAY command, 48
displaying
file contents, 120-121
information, 118-119
DO CASE, ENDCASE command,
49-50
DO command, 48
DO WHILE, ENDDO command,
50-51
DOS prompt, performing
operations from, 101-102
dot prompt, stopping program
and returning to, 99-100
DROP DATABASE SQL
command, 140
DROP INDEX SQL
command, 140
DROP SYNONYM SQL
command, 140
DROP TABLE SQL
command, 140
DROP VIEW SQL
command, 140

E

EDIT command, 51-53
EJECT, EJECT PAGE
command, 53-54
ENDIF command, 61-62
ending current session, 73, 87
ENDSCAN command, 103-104
ENDTEXT command, 118-119
ERASE command, 54-55
errors, trapping, 76-78
ESCAPE command, 76-77
EXPORT command, 55-56

F

FETCH INTO SQL
command, 141
fields
filling with blanks, 14
finding key fields, 57-58
memo, reading files into,
11-12
numeric, 119-120
replacing with data stored
in arrays, 93
restricting access, 85-86
updating, 122-123
files
creating
Binary Named List
(BNL), 46
from non-dBASE
software, 63
displaying contents,
120-121
integrity tag, resetting,
95-96
listing, 47-48
locks, releasing, 121-122
multiple index files,
removing tags from,
45-46
names, changing, 90-91
reading into memo fields,
11-12
removing from disk
without ending session,
54-55
searching, 104-105
for specific values,
72-73
FIND command, 57-58
flagging records, 44-45
FUNCTION command, 58
function syntax, 126
functions, 126-136
low-level file I/O functions,
137-138

G-H

GO command, 59-60
GOTO command, 59-60
GRANT ALL ON TO PUBLIC SQL command, 141
HELP command, 60-61

I

IF command, 61-62
IMPORT command, 63
INDEX command, 64-65
INSERT INTO SQL command, 141
INSERT INTO VALUES SQL command, 141
integrity tag, resetting, 95-96

J-K

JOIN command, 66-68
KEY command, 76-77
KEYBOARD command, 68
keys, recognizing, 76-77

L

LABEL FORM command, 68-69
LIST command, 69-71
LOAD command, 71
LOAD DATA FROM INTO TABLE SQL command, 141
LOCATE command, 72-73
LOGOUT command, 73
low-level file I/O functions, 137-138

M

macros, playing, 81-82
memo fields, reading files into, 11-12
memory, removing information, 21
menus
  bounce bar, building, 39-40
  pop-up, 77-78
MODIFY APPLICATION command, 73
MODIFY COMMAND/FILE command, 74
MODIFY LABEL command, 74
MODIFY QUERY/VIEW command, 75
MODIFY REPORT command, 75
MODIFY SCREEN command, 75
MODIFY STRUCTURE command, 75
MOVE WINDOW command, 75
moving record pointer
  within databases, 112-113
  within datafiles, 59-60
multiple index files, removing tags, 45-46

N-O

numeric fields, summing values, 119-120
ON ERROR command, 76-77
ON PAD command, 77-78
ON PAGE command, 78
ON READERROR command, 78
ON SELECTION PAD command, 79
ON SELECTION POPUP command, 79
OPEN SQL command, 141
opening datafiles, 123-124

P

PACK command, 79
PARAMETERS command, 79-81
passing values, 79-81
PLAY MACRO command, 81-82
pop-up menus, 77-78
positioning the cursor, 3-5
printers
  moving paper to top of next page, 53-54
  sending information, 69-71
printing
  controlling printing activity, 82-83

labels for open datafiles, 29-30, 68-69
PRINTJOB/ENDPRINTJOB commands, 82-83
PRIVATE command, 83-84
PROCEDURE command, 85
programs
binary, running, 18-19
changing, 36-37
from readable source code to object code, 23-24
controlling flow base on data values, 49-50
dBASE IV
changing, 74
running, 48
executing again after error detection, 98-99
performing multiple command lines within, 103-104
resuming, 97-98
sections of performing specialized tasks, 58
stopping
and closing, 19-20
asking user for information, 6-7, 65
returning to dot prompt, 99-100
suspending execution, 117-118
testing new programs, 36-37
writing
in sections, 85
with Applications Generator, 27-28
PROTECT command, 85-86
PUBLIC command, 87

Q-R

QUIT command, 87
READ command, 88
RECALL command, 88-89
record
maintenance screens, 33-34
pointer, moving
in databases, 112-113
within datafile, 59-60
records
adding
to databases, 9-10
to datafiles, 8-9
calculating, 17-18
copying, 25-27
extracting from datafiles, 30-31
filling with blanks, 14
flagging for removal in datafiles, 44-45
inserting into datafiles, 66
organizing, 113-114
printing from open datafiles, 32-33
removing
all records in datafiles, 125
deletion flags for, 88-89
REINDEX command, 89
RELEASE command, 89-90
RENAME command, 90-91
REPLACE command, 91-93
REPLACE FROM ARRAY command, 93
REPORT FORM command, 94-95
reports, defining boxes, 38-39
RESET command, 95-96
RESTORE command, 96
restricting access to dBASE IV, 85-86
RESUME command, 97-98
RETRY command, 98-99
RETURN command, 99-100
REVOKE ALL FROM PUBLIC/SQL command, 141
ROLLBACK command, 100
ROLLBACK SQL command, 141
RUN/! command, 101-102
running dBASE IV programs, 48
RUNSTATS SQL command, 141

S

SAVE command, 102-103
SCAN command, 103-104
screens
  activating entire screen, 7-8
  Browse, 33-34
  Control Center, 12
  defining areas of, 42-43
  manipulating, 5-6
  record maintenance, 33-34
  removing information, 21
  sending information, 69-71
searching files, 104-105
SEEK command, 104-105
SELECT command, 106
SELECT SQL command, 142
selecting work areas for database files, 106
sending dBASE IV data to other software packages, 55-56
SET command, 107-112
SHOW DATABASE SQL command, 142
SHOW MENU command, 112
SHOW POPUP command, 112
SKIP command, 112-113
SORT command, 113-114
SQL commands, 139-142
START DATABASE SQL command, 142
STOP DATABASE SQL command, 142
stopping programs, 19-20
  asking user for information, 6-7
STORE command, 114-117
SUM command, 117
SUSPEND command, 117-118

T

TEXT command, 118-119
TOTAL command, 119-120
TYPE command, 120-121
type-ahead keyboard buffer, 68

U-V

UNLOAD DATA TO FROM TABLE SQL command, 142
UNLOCK command, 121-122
UPDATE command, 122-123
UPDATE SET SQL command, 142
UPDATE SET WHERE CURRENT OF SQL command, 142
updating fields, 122-123
USE command, 123-124
values, passing, 79-81

W-Z

WAIT command, 124
windows containing messages/borders, 41-42
work areas, selecting for database files, 106
ZAP command, 125